MEMPHIS TO MADAGASCAR

MY LIFE IN FOCUS

MEMPHIS TO MADAGASCAR

MY LIFE IN FOCUS

BILL HURD, M.D.

Copyright © 2025 Bill Hurd, M.D.

All rights reserved. No part of this book may be reproduced in any form without written permission from the publisher.

The photographs included in *Memphis to Madagascar: My Life in Focus* help bring the stories to life, and we are deeply grateful to everyone who contributed to this visual collection. Every effort has been made to credit all images appropriately. If you happen to recognize a photo and have more information about its source, we'd love to hear from you so we can make any necessary updates in future editions.

Published by Soulstir Books, a division of Soulstir LLC
12412 Bittersweet Commons Blvd W #365, Granger, Indiana 46530
soulstirbooks.com

Soulstir Books and Soulstir are trademarks or registered trademarks of Soulstir LLC.

Editing by David Parker Jr. and Jada Norris
Book design by Michelle Mayhall

Hardcover ISBN: 979-8-9850370-9-8

Printed and bound in the United States of America.
First Edition 9 8 7 6 5 4 3 2 1

CONTENTS

Prologue   vii

Part I Growing Up   1

Chapter 1 My Family   3
Chapter 2 Discovering Talents   10
Chapter 3 High School Education and Social Life   17
Chapter 4 One Tenth of a Second   31

Part II University of Notre Dame   43

Chapter 5 Settling In   45
Chapter 6 Shenanigans   54
Chapter 7 The Need for Speed   63
Chapter 8 Football and Music   71
Chapter 9 Social Life, Social Issues, & Olympics   77

Part III 1969-1980   87

Chapter 10 Boston   89
Chapter 11 Nashville   102
Chapter 12 Medical School   109

Part IV Returning Home as Bill Hurd, M.D.   119

Chapter 13 Internship and Residency   121

Chapter 14 Medical Practice   130

Part V World-Wide Mission Trips   137

Chapter 15 Medical Missions   139

Chapter 16 Madagascar   143

Part VI Retirement   151

Chapter 17 The End Is Just the Beginning   153

Chapter 18 Notre Dame Reconnections   159

Chapter 19 Family Pride and Sorrow   163

Chapter 20 What If   172

Epilogue   179

A Life in Focus: Photos and Memories from the Journey   183

Awards, Honors, and Distinctions   207

PROLOGUE

I believe that life is a gift and an ever-evolving journey. My journey began in Memphis, Tennessee, and eventually took me to Madagascar, an island off the southeast coast of Africa, and other faraway regions of the world. Throughout this journey, I have developed and nurtured technical abilities, musical talents, and surgical skills. As I look back, my life's path has come into sharp focus, and certain moments stand out like landmarks: events that changed my fortunes, for better or worse, experiences that changed me and the way I see the world, and efforts to make positive changes in my own small ways.

Here's one such moment. March 1987. In the sweltering heat of an abandoned school building in a small village in Madagascar, I performed more than 30 cataract surgeries in a makeshift, poorly ventilated surgery site. Most often, cataracts develop with age, ultimately leading to blindness if untreated. Many people's worlds are reduced to a shadowy existence where they only experience the most basic detection of motion or light. They can't even count their own fingers. The only remedy for an advanced cataract is to surgically remove the clouded lens and replace it with a lens implant, and that's what I was here to do in Madagascar. Despite limited running water and resources, the possibilities and the energy in the air felt infinite as lines of patients gathered and their hopes grew for a chance at improved vision—and life. Many patients who had traveled miles to receive this procedure showered the medical team with gifts of food and offerings from their own gardens and farms. Imagine the atmosphere in a room full of quiet villagers who have come from afar bearing gifts and are all patiently waiting to be treated by a foreign eye surgeon for the very first time. I quickly realized there were far more people than I would have time to care for, and the vast majority of the patients had advanced cataracts in both eyes. To restore vision to as many people as possible, I decided to perform surgery on just one of their eyes.

Every patient I treated during this trip remains woven into the fabric of my life, yet one particular woman stands out vividly. An elderly Malagasy woman had traveled miles by foot to reach me despite being almost completely blind. Neatly dressed in her colorful garments, she waited with a stoic expression on her face for a chance to reclaim her vision. She had lived in darkness and shadows for years, her family slowly fading from sight while her cataracts progressed. After her surgery, when I finally removed the gauze from her surgically repaired eye, emotion surfaced on her face for the first time since I met her. The stoic look melted away, and tears streamed down her cheeks. When an assistant asked why she was crying, she stated in the local dialect of Madagascar that she could now see her small grandchild for the first time. I was so happy for this elderly woman and glad to help bring about such a life-changing event. I usually maintain a friendly but professional demeanor around patients, and I did not intend to expose my own emotions, but after seeing her tears of joy, I cried, too.

Being able to restore eyesight was one of the reasons I chose ophthalmology as my specialty after medical school. At the time, I had not even considered how I would be able to transport my surgical skills from a hospital or private office setting to a grossly underserved place like Madagascar, but this turned out to be an unforeseen advantage of my specialty. To experience moments like I did with this Malagasy woman, where joy and tears come together, was extremely rewarding for me. I am reminded even today of the importance of being able to laugh and cry and feel the full spectrum of human emotion on a daily basis. This particular trip to Madagascar was one of many trips I took in the 1980s and 1990s, working with teams of physicians to deliver care in rural and underserved parts of Mexico, Brazil, South Africa, West Africa, and Madagascar. The story of the elderly Malagasy woman regaining her eyesight was one of many, yet we never took for granted how important every single surgery was to the patients we saw.

In this memoir, I want to tell the story of how a young Black kid from the segregated inner city of North Memphis grew up to perform eye surgery on the other side of the world as part of a series of medical missions. As expected, this journey was not without obstacles along the way. Racism, tokenism, hatred, and isolation often plagued my academic and career efforts. Being a musician helped me deal with adversity. Music has always been a running theme in my life and continues to contribute to my mental health and stability. Facing these obstacles made me stronger and smarter, putting me in a better position to survive through any adversity. Not only were closed doors in front of me forced open but they were left open for generations to follow.

Along the way, many people changed the course of my life, whether they were friends or foes, whether they supported me through the joys and trials of life or created obstacles that I learned from. And now, by reliving my journey from Memphis to Madagascar and back, I have the unique opportunity to put my life in a new focus and see the larger arc of it.

PART I
GROWING UP

CHAPTER 1

MY FAMILY

I grew up in an all-Black community in Memphis, Tennessee, in the late 50's and early 60's, when segregation was strictly enforced. My neighbors were family friends, and everyone chipped in to raise the children. I was born May 17, 1947, to Leon Hurd Sr. and Doris Parker Hurd. The third child of four, I followed behind my older brother, Leon Hurd, Jr, and my older sister, Avar Hurd James. My younger sister is Mildred Hurd Langston-Hemphill. My father was a letter carrier for the United States Postal Service, and my mother was a stay-at-home mom. Leon Jr., who we called Lil' Leon, was the big brother I needed for advice, support, and protection from bullies. During our adolescence, I really looked up to him, both literally and figuratively. He always seemed to be two or three inches taller than me. It was great having a big brother. He was very protective and also proud to have me as his little brother, especially as my athletic career evolved. Avar, who we affectionately called Sista, was the sibling who kept the rest of us from getting out of line. Mildred, five years younger than me, was not quite old enough to be involved in my adolescent experiences. Like most others in our neighborhood, we grew up in a close-knit family in an area of north Memphis called Scutterfield, bordered by Chelsea Avenue to the south, Thomas Street to the west, Firestone Avenue to the north, and Morehead Street to the east. Single parenting was rare, and crime, unemployment, and drug addiction were relatively low. It was socially acceptable for a neighborhood adult to discipline a child not of his or her own family. The phrase "It takes a village to raise a child" could have been the unofficial motto of my neighborhood.

My sister, Avar; My brother, Leon Jr.

Our two-story house was modest but not unlike the other houses on Manassas Street, three blocks from the school. My dad and his friends later built a den adjacent to the living room and a one-car garage at the end of the driveway. Upstairs, Leon and I shared one of two small bedrooms, and Sista and Mildred shared the other. A large closet completed the second-floor layout. I can still picture this setting because my dad would often come upstairs to say goodnight, and I was the only one with the light on past bedtime, working puzzles or trying to solve math problems.

It was the kind of community where neighbors often became extensions of your own family. I can recall playing flag football in Rochester Neely's backyard and anticipating the huge tuna fish sandwiches his mother would always prepare for us after our playtime. Or being invited by Dr. Art Horne, Sr. to tag along with his son Art Jr. to play golf at Fullers Golf Course, which was the only nice golf course in Memphis for Black people at that time. The close-knit community fostered a lifelong trust among the neighborhood families, so much so that most of them would become my clinical patients later in life.

Despite the fond memories of my childhood growing up in Memphis, I would be remiss to forget the unpleasant experiences of prejudice that plagued my life. Living in the Jim Crow South as a young Black child was a unique experience that blended the sense of community and safety that Black neighborhoods provided with the fear, isolation, and "otherness" of the world outside of it. There was no way around the racism of the time, and it seeped into every fiber of life, whether it was consciously perceived or not. This was also a time of change, and social dynamics were transforming in many parts of the nation, even if they were only grudgingly accepted by many white Americans. In 1954, the Supreme Court handed down the Brown v. Board of Education decision that led to the integration of schools. In 1955, Rosa Parks refused to give up her bus seat to a white man. Yet much of the South still felt stagnant and immobile. As an adolescent growing up with institutional as well as social racism and segregation, it was difficult to determine what was normal and what was not. Only years later, when I left home and interacted with people from all over the world, would I realize the full extent of those challenges.

My dad did his best not only to protect us but also to prepare us. He often reminded my siblings and me at an early age that we would have to work twice as hard for a position due to our skin color, and even then, we might not receive it. This sounded daunting for a young Black kid. Social changes were always around the corner, but my little corner of the South seemed to refuse the change. I drank out of public water fountains with signs above them that read: "For Colored Only." I was required to sit at the back of buses or trains. My parents were often disrespected by racist white people in positions of authority, right in the presence of their children.

My mom, Doris

My parents were two people who seemed in sync even during the most trying times, though they each handled the pressure and injustice of racism in vastly different ways. My mom, Doris, who most people viewed as a sweet and soft-spoken lady, would often fume about such incidents, referring to racists as "nasty peckerwoods," while my father maintained a relatively level head and did not react adversely to such racist encounters. Much later, during my older adolescence and adult life, I found myself mirroring my father's more reserved emotional temperament when confronted with racism and other forms of adversity. I used the internalized anger to push forward and stay focused on whatever was in my line of sight.

One of the first jobs I was offered as a child was picking cotton during the summer harvest season in the nearby cotton fields of western Tennessee and northern Mississippi. It was grueling work, and the pay was no better than it had been for the sharecroppers of the 1800s. Decent, good-paying summer jobs for youngsters like me were limited, however, so when my neighborhood buddy, Jerry Peterson, encouraged me to join him at his summer job in the cotton fields, I considered it carefully. We would be picked up at sunrise in a school bus and deposited in the fields until sunset for less than $5.00 per day. I vehemently declined, figuring there must be a better way to make a few bucks during the hot and humid Memphis summer months.

It took some time, but patience paid off when I was able to get a newspaper route instead. I delivered copies of the Memphis Press Scimitar in the mornings and mowed my neighbors' lawns in the evenings. At this stage of my childhood, I wasn't even aware of the full negative implications of Black people picking cotton on a plantation. The history of slavery was not taught in the Memphis school system, and I did not learn until much later that slaves, including quite possibly, my own ancestors, were forced to pick cotton from sunup to sundown in the extreme mid-southern humid heat, possibly on the very same cotton plantations that my neighborhood buddies worked.

I remember watching the movie *Amistad* years later, which portrayed the transport of slaves in the mid-1800s from West Africa to the Americas, and I was absolutely astonished to see and learn this history. Nothing like this was taught in my high school. Still later, on one of my medical mission trips to Senegal, I made a point to visit the slave houses on Gorée Island, just off the coast of Dakar, Senegal. There was an uncomfortable and eerie stillness in the air as Dr. Lawrence Madlock and I looked at each other while standing in the middle of one of these concrete slave houses. This was the very place where male slaves were shackled before entering the "Point of No Return" and boarded ships like the Amistad. Dr. Madlock and I looked around, knowing quite likely that our ancestors had been confined within these very walls.

To this day, the word plantation still does not sit well with me. I would frown when my golf buddies had a tee time to play at Plantation Golf Course in Olive Branch, Mississippi, which was eventually renamed Timber Truss Golf Course. When my wife Rhynette and I would search for a new home, we would always cross off any neighborhood with the word "plantation" in it. We did not like to be reminded constantly of this ugly aspect of American history or the millions upon millions of people who died in bondage in those work camps and even more during the hundreds of voyages in the Trans Atlantic Slave Trade between the 1500's to the 1800's. Estimates for the number of enslaved Africans forcibly brought to the Americas range from ten to twelve million. It is no wonder why there is resistance to include this horrific human behavior in our American history textbooks.

Despite the hardships of living in the South during the 1960s, the lessons and experiences I gained were invaluable. They sparked a drive in me. They inspired me to break through the glass ceiling and strive for a meaningful and worthwhile life. I am thankful for my family and the individuals I met along the way, who encouraged me to reach new heights and never to accept the limitations placed before me.

CHAPTER 2
DISCOVERING TALENTS

Here's another moment. The summer of 1959. Kansas City, Missouri, where my grandmother lived. In the crippling afternoon heat, sweat ran down my face as I hopped fences, ducked under trees, and sprinted faster than I ever knew possible. This was not a childhood competition between friends but a race for survival as a huge brown German Shepherd chased me down the street, snarling and clipping at my heels. I ran through the neighborhood, hoping for someone to save me from what I was sure would be a brutal mauling. No one came. I was alone with the sounds of my shoes touching the pavement, my own heavy breathing, and the dog. The only thing that would save me at this point was figuring out how to stay one yard ahead of this beast. I saw the fence of my grandmother's house come into view, and a surge of hope gave me one last boost of speed. I covered that final stretch and dove over those white pickets into the safety of her small yard as my family and friends looked on with astonishment all over their faces. "William," said my brother, Leon

Jr. "You are *fast*." Hopping that fence achieved two things for me that summer: notoriety among my family and friends and a newly discovered athletic ability that would change my life. What was initially a traumatic event ended up revealing a God-given gift of foot speed.

We often spent our summers in Kansas City at the home of my grandmother, Avar Pipkin, or Mah-Mah, as we affectionately called her. We looked forward to these summer trips with great anticipation. The train ride from Memphis felt exciting, and we loved these opportunities to be away from our parents, form new friendships, and follow new adventures. I can still taste the cold fried chicken sandwich my mom had prepared for us for the long train ride from Memphis to Kansas City. There were several families where she lived on Spruce Street near Swope Park that had children our ages. There was the Herndon family of four boys and one girl. Leon Jr. and I spent a lot of time at the Herndon household, one street over from Mah-Mah's, since there were guys there our age. The Peterson family, who lived on the end of Spruce Street, consisted of Dr Carl Peterson, his wife, and their two sons, Carl Jr. and Louis. The summers in Kansas led to lifelong friendships with people that often encouraged my success and even saved lives in my family. Louis would go on to become a pediatrician, and his father, Dr. Carl Peterson, a general surgeon, performed life-saving colon cancer surgery on my grandmother that extended her life by thirty-three years and allowed her to celebrate her ninety-ninth birthday before she passed.

Avar Pipkin was born in rural Oakland, Tennessee, in 1906 and died in 2005. She spent her entire life in the South, raised at the height of racism. Despite the limitations enforced on Black Americans during this time, Avar strived for a life beyond this and established herself as a savvy business woman despite her lack of formal education. Being a dedicated, God-fearing woman, she took us to church every Sunday we spent with her. My grandmother's dedication to Christianity remained the solid foundation of her belief system and inspired her and others to achieve the impossible for Black folks living in the Jim Crow era. Mah-Mah's faith in the church was unbreakable and, at times, conflicted with modernity and growth. On April 13, 1977, during my first year in medical school at Meharry, I received a phone call from my mother relaying the unfortunate message that my grandmother was diagnosed with early-stage colon cancer by our trusted family friend, Dr. Peterson. Her immediate plan was to do nothing and just "put her fate in God's hands." Upon hearing this, I quickly got on the telephone with her. After a lengthy conversation, I convinced her to have the non-metastatic colon tumor surgically removed.

My grandmother, Avar Pipkin

In her later years, Mah-Mah moved from Kansas City to Bartlett, a suburb north of Memphis, to reside with my widowed mom, Doris. She bragged to her church members and friends about her grandson, who was now a surgeon, and when she eventually needed cataract surgery of her own, she refused to allow any other ophthalmologist to perform it for her. While performing surgery on your own family members is not uncommon, many surgeons that I know avoided doing surgical procedures or even administering medical treatment to family members. Some consider it taboo. The pressure surrounding physicians performing medical procedures on family members can also be problematic. Plus, it can lead to anxiety and even, on rare occasions, to mistakes by the treating physician. However, my grandmother insisted, and in the end, I was pleased to help restore her vision back to normal. My grandmother is long gone, but I still remember the words she spoke to me before her surgery, "I trust your steady hands, William."

I always had a drive to pursue whatever goals I put my mind to, but there were moments that helped me get a glimpse of how far these goals might take me if I allowed them to. One summer afternoon, my father and I were engaged in one of our frequent checkers games. I was thirteen when my father took this occasion to tell me he thought I had special gifts. To hear this from my father, a man I admired, was a wonderful moment between us. It signified to me that my father believed in me and saw a bright future for me. He saw something that I was still too young to envision, but his words made me aware of a light way out on the horizon—and made me feel like I could reach it. The bond between my father and me was irrevocable. I really loved my dad more than anyone else. At times, it seemed like we were mirror images of each other. During those checker games, we often discussed my interest in track, academics, and music. I would occasionally beat him. My father was never bothered by losing to me but was impressed with my ability to beat him at such a young age.

My dad, Leon Sr.

I never shared the conversations between my father and myself with my brother and sisters, fearing it would create unnecessary friction. I didn't want my dad to be accused of showing favoritism, even though I did believe I was the favored child among my siblings. My parents loved all of us and avoided any preferential treatment; however, as a child, I felt the weight of these increased expectations. For me, this duty came with the responsibility and extra motivation to be a good kid and stay out of trouble, an enormous amount of self-imposed pressure for a thirteen-year-old. It didn't help that everyone in the neighborhood referred to me as my dad's twin, both in stature and personality. He was my role model, and I aspired to be just like him. He was athletic, a musician, a good provider, and a caring father and husband. I believed my dad could do everything well. I saw how nice he was to people and that everyone who knew him loved him. In addition to his full-time work with the postal service, he played trumpet in church and in the letter-carriers band and was a very resourceful and skilled handyman. Our neighbors would seek his services, sometimes to my mom's dismay, further exemplifying the notion of "love thy neighbor." I never heard him say anything bad about anyone or anyone say anything bad about him. He lived a life worth aspiring to, and I only hoped that I could measure up as time went along.

When I think back to my earliest opportunities, it was really my father who opened many of those doors. His approval, love, and encouragement gave me the right amount of courage to blaze through the obstacles set before me. I am blessed to have had the father-son bond that encapsulated my life up until my father's rest. He never told me he loved me, but as I got older and had my own children, I realized my father did not have to verbalize his love because I constantly felt it. The selfless acts of my father inspired me with my own sons, and I strive to demonstrate this and show my sons I love them at every opportunity. And while I don't regret that my father did not verbalize his affections, that is something I wanted to do for my own family. The joy of saying and hearing "I love you" was something I wanted in my home. I learned that you should not just silently love the people you care about; you should tell them. Do it often and with sincerity.

CHAPTER 3
HIGH SCHOOL EDUCATION AND SOCIAL LIFE

With my family's unwavering support and help from wonderfully devoted Manassas High teachers, I developed a strong focus on academics through my middle and high school years. I found myself enjoying school, with a passion for science and math that overshadowed all other subjects. It was not uncommon to find me at my desk in the late hours of the night, trying to solve extracurricular math problems given to me by my math teachers, Ms. Turner and Ms. Parker, or tackling math problems published in MIT's monthly magazine. Solving problems was an adrenaline rush; failing and trying again and again until you finally achieved the answer was exciting. MIT published a monthly magazine that allowed readers to submit their own solutions to difficult math problems. This exposed me to more advanced math topics not taught in my high school. On one occasion, when I was a junior, I submitted my own solution to a math problem that was published in their next issue.

My close friend and classmate, Edward Lee Thompson, and I often engaged in constructive and recreational academic competition, especially in Advanced Placement courses. We also enjoyed many hours of each other's company, studying together and ending our study sessions with card games. These kinds of friendships allowed me to express my "nerdy" side in high school without judgment. Despite the inevitable presence of a few school bullies who target nerds as their victim, my saving grace was that I was also a known athlete. I feel lucky to have had a community of family and friends that respected that nerdy side of me and allowed me to expand and enjoy my interests and hobbies.

Math became the calming resolution in my life. It scratched the constant itch in my brain for stability and rationalization. For me, if you are able to solve a math problem successfully, there is no debate on the final answer. Despite the different approaches or solutions to a given math problem, the answer is constant. This characteristic of math was always intriguing, I thought. Perhaps it was my love of math that led to my analytical approach to solving problems more generally. Different approaches can lead to the same correct outcome. At the same time, I tended to shy away from more subjective topics. For example, if I were to ask you to describe a flower vase, you could potentially give an infinite number of polysyllabic descriptions of its color, shape, size, etc. On the other hand, if I ask you to determine the volume of the same flower vase, given its dimensions, there is only one non-debatable answer for its volume. As I matured as a young adult, I concluded that I favored issues defined by objectivity over subjectivity. After the final performance of an Olympic gymnast, a set of judges tally their scores to determine the final winner of the competition. I would rather watch an Olympic 800-meter final where the gold, silver, and bronze medal winners don't require judges to determine the outcome. Judges introduce both human error and personal attitude, two things that most sports spectators don't want to see. The introduction of technology and artificial intelligence into the sports arena has already made a positive impact by reducing bad or missed referee calls with instant replay, or determining instantly if a tennis ball is in or out of bounds during a grand slam tennis match. Similar technology, robotics and A.I. will continue to infiltrate our daily lives with the intent of reducing laborious and repetitive tasks like driving a car or going to the post office or bank. In theory, this will allow more time to be creative and perhaps more importantly, learn how to live with and respect each other despite our differences in culture and skin color. This is not just theory; it is also hope.

    In 1956, I came to Manassas High School as a third grader. During the 1950s and 1960s, it was not unusual for Black students in Memphis inner city schools, like Booker T. Washington and Manassas High School, to attend the same school for the entire 12 years. I came to Manassas as a third grader from Carnes Elementary. My time at Manassas High School allowed me to flourish in many different ways.

    Manassas High School did not have many of the luxuries that White high schools had in Memphis. We had to use hand-me-down books, and we did not have a track field or a full football field to train on or develop our athletic skills. There were only a handful of golf courses or tennis courts available for Blacks in the whole city, as most of those were tucked away in private country clubs with White-only facilities. Academic and sports programs were underfunded or simply nonexistent at Black schools. I often wonder how many remarkable talents were cast to the wayside due to this structural racism. There were so many talented individuals and not enough opportunity. This is something I believe still plagues the Black community. When an entire generation is held down, it severely limits what they are able to pass on to the next generation. On a more positive note, our Manassas teachers and principals were remarkably skillful, dedicated and encouraging.

What we had was a drive to succeed and some dedicated and incredibly caring teachers and coaches. Despite the lack of support from the state, Manassas was able to produce generations of top students, athletes, musicians, and legacies. Against this backdrop, my own athletic career began. Knowing how fast I was, my friends and family urged me to join the track team, and I didn't need much encouragement. I had discovered that I loved being fast. I loved the physicality of running and being able to compete. I quickly found my place on the team, training hard and developing my sprinting skills under a skilled coaching staff that included track coaches Bubba Jennings and Emmit Simon.

Since we didn't have a track, we trained on a makeshift dirt field outside the Firestone Tire plant. We used rocks or chunks of wood for starting blocks and spent hours running through the foul-smelling fumes that wafted out of that adjacent Firestone factory full of vulcanized rubber. Despite these harsh conditions, I would look forward to track practice because I realized that I could get better. Every day after school, I wanted to be in that terrible field, running. Getting faster. Getting out of the starting blocks quicker.

It got to the point where I even hated to be out of school for holidays. Well, at least the less significant holidays. I wanted to be in school as much as possible, where I could learn something new and race to the track field after the final bell. As a teenager, I knew I was self-motivated, but I didn't recognize that I was also developing valuable study and practice habits that would become the bedrock of a long, successful career and life. Of course, these habits also inspired my classmates to give me the title of "nerd," something I was able to wear as a badge of honor. In my 1965 Manassas senior yearbook, I was voted "Most Studious" and "Mr. Brains." Rather than taking any of this as an insult, these titles made me hopeful for the future.

I was proud of my academic and sports achievements so far, but my true love has always centered around music. I had been surrounded by music my whole life, especially as my father and his jazz band, The Letter Carriers, held practices and rehearsals at our house. My father played the trumpet, and my childhood afternoons and evenings were filled with the sweet, soulful music of jazz, filling the house from one end to the other. I would watch my father and his friends—who all worked for the U.S. postal service—play, dreaming of a chance to be part of a band. The comradery mixed with the artistic creation that can only come from a group of artists working together was something to behold. I also spent hours listening to saxophonists John Coltrane, Cannonball Adderly, and Charlie "Bird" Parker, paying special attention to their improvised solos.

So, when I lifted my very first instrument, an alto saxophone that dad bought for me, I took to it instantly. The school band room felt like a home away from home. I quickly progressed and began playing three different instruments in the three different school bands: alto saxophone in the jazz band, oboe in the concert band, and clarinet in the marching band. Much like mathematics, I found music to be fascinating, soothing, and endlessly rewarding. In a musical form like jazz, I discovered that here, too, you could find numerous paths to reach the same bridge or destination.

By the time I reached the 8th grade, I was the youngest student to make the varsity band. By my junior year, I played the first chair oboe in the Tennessee state-wide band—an incredible honor. All this, I achieved under the direction of the legendary band director Emerson Able. Fortunately for me, he also was a gifted saxophonist who became a mentor. Perhaps most significantly, Emerson Able was single-handedly responsible for hundreds of Manassas graduates getting college educations on music scholarships between 1956 and 1971. Emerson Able was later awarded a prestigious Note on Beale Street in downtown Memphis, a ceremony I could not miss.

Of everything I was passionate about, music soon became my favorite extracurricular activity. I spent hours honing my skills and defining my jazz sound on the alto saxophone. At home, my family forced me to take my annoyingly long practice sessions to our garage, which my dad and his friends had built by hand, pouring the foundation and laying every brick. It smelled of concrete and mortar, but surprisingly, I felt like the acoustics enhanced my sound. An echo and reverb effect colored the notes coming out of my saxophone. All the stresses in my young life seemed to melt away as the sweet harmonic music filled the garage. Jazz became the soothing balm to the harsh realities of adolescence, racism, and growing pains. I could feel my frustrations fade away as I poured my heart and soul into whatever I was playing. I felt closer to myself, my father, and, strangely, the universe.

One afternoon, my dad asked me to fill in on the alto sax for The Letter Carriers. Their regular saxophonist was an impressive player, but, unfortunately, he was unable to make it to the upcoming show. I did not think I was ready to play at this level with professional musicians, but my dad knew I was ready. After all these years of watching and listening, I knew the songs by heart, and my skills had developed after all those hours in the garage. On the night of the show, my stomach was twisted into nervous knots, but I followed my father's steady lead as we took the stage. Looking out at the room full of people, I couldn't believe this was really happening. But by the time we launched into "Giant Steps" by John Coltrane, I was lost in the music, immersed in the flow of the band. It was the greatest night of my young life. It was another of my father's amazing gifts to me.

Back in the school jazz band, I strived to keep developing my skills. I played second alto saxophone behind one of my mentors, Herbert Smith, who played first alto sax. Smith, who later became Director of Jazz Studies at Southern Illinois University (1970 to 1974), then Director of Jazz Studies at Howard University in Washington D.C., followed by the same position at Northern Virginia Community College, had a sweet, smooth alto sound that reminded me of altoist Paul Desmond and attracted my attention. So, I frequently picked his brain, and he was gracious enough to accept my request to practice with him at his home. Herbert, along with his younger brother, Coby, and mother, Lula Smith, were close to the Hurds since both have family ties to Oakland, Tennessee, in Fayette County.

Coby also turned out to be influential in my life, though for different reasons. A year my senior, he was a natural student leader and later a prominent local civil rights activist who I admired. As a senior, he was the student body president and the student cadet lieutenant colonel battalion commander of the National Defense Cadet Corp (NDCC), which was a forerunner to the modern Junior Reserve Officers Training Corp (JROTC). The NDCC was prominent in the Black Memphis schools. Following Coby's lead, my NDCC experience led to my becoming his cadet major, the second in command in my junior year. After he graduated, I became the student cadet lieutenant colonel battalion commander myself. I took this high school military experience seriously because I saw how it promoted discipline, leadership, and teamwork. I also served as senior class president during my last year at Manassas.

Along with the artistic brainstorming that existed in the Manassas music scene, there were several competitive talent shows known as "Annual Shows" that fueled the magnetic air of

1960s Black jazz communities. In the 1960 "Annual Show" in the Manassas auditorium, I watched a tall 6'6" Frank McRae sing the song "You Better Stop Doggin' Me Around" (popularized by the late singer Jackie Wilson) using his projectile tenor of a voice that captivated me and the rest of the student audience. Frank graduated from Manassas in 1960 and went on to play in the NFL, followed by a successful acting career in American film and television. He appeared in "48 Hours", starring Nick Nolte and Eddie Murphy, and "Paradise Alley" starring Sylvester Stallone. Frank died in 2021 at age 80.

Music played a role in introducing me to my future wife, Rhynette. Meeting her for the first time is another moment etched into my memory. On a cold fall evening after classes during my junior year, I was in the band room practicing on my saxophone. As I played, a cool breeze suddenly swept in, and I looked up to find the door open. I stopped playing, curious about who else would be entering the band room at this hour. To my surprise, a pretty girl stood at the door, her petite frame wrapped in an overcoat. Standing next to her was a familiar face, Thurman Northcross, a sophomore, who turned out to be her older brother.

Rhynette asked Thurman who I was, and as our eyes connected, something magical sparked between us. Remember, I was a total nerd at this time, completely absorbed in my music, schoolwork, and track practice. I had little interest in girls, and my shyness only compounded the situation. Eventually, however, we struck up a conversation and began to see each other regularly. I met Rhynette's parents, Verdell and Thurman Sr., and I would occasionally attend Parkway Gardens Presbyterian Church with her family. It also felt comforting to know that the Hurd and Northcross families were connected through our fathers, who were both U.S. postal workers.

My participation in the various bands under the direction of Mr. Emerson Able combined with being a significant member of the track team came with some conflicting scheduling. Even as a teenager I could sense the frustration from Mr. Able by my missing band practices because of conflicting track practice and track meets. There was an incident that illustrates my dilemma of being in the band and on the track team simultaneously.

The Manassas concert band was performing in an all-state band competition in Nashville on a Friday afternoon. We had travelled by bus. It was my sophomore year. I was playing first chair oboe and we were awarded first place in the state-wide event. But there was a very important all-regional track meet in Memphis beginning Saturday morning, the next day. Nashville and Memphis are 200 miles apart and the three and a half hour trip by car was neither practical nor possible. What happened next was an amazing display of teamwork and unselfishness. My track coaches, Bubba Jennings and Emmit Simon, the football coach Johnny Johnson and the basketball coach Charles Thompson all chipped in and purchased a one-way airplane ticket for me to fly from Nashville to Memphis in time for me to compete in the Saturday morning regional track meet. I never forgot that kind gesture. For me, it was the very first time I had flown in an airplane. Years later after I had established myself in the medical field, I made it a point to show my appreciation to each of these men, especially to Mr. Bubba Jennings. Although we finished in 2nd place in the regional track meet at the Fairgrounds track facility, my individual performance made a difference.

The downside of this whole ordeal was a deterioration of my relationship with Mr. Able, who forced me to choose between the band and track. Consequently, I was not a part of the school band the second half of my junior year and all of my senior year. However I continued to practice on my alto saxophone at home and "sit-in" on gigs at jazz and R&B clubs around town at every opportunity. The good news is that years later, Mr. Able and I became very close friends, as I visited him frequently at his home. He was also a patient in my clinical practice.

My junior year ended on a bright June afternoon, and all the students poured out excitedly into what was sure to be a hot Memphis summer. I had a lot to be proud of and grateful for as I pushed out through those doors with my friends and schoolmates: straight A's on my report card, a first-place finish in the 100-yard dash at the 1964 all-Black Tennessee segregated state track meet, and a trip to Nashville where I performed in the all-state concert band and played first chair oboe. There was no time to rest on my laurels, though. I was already preparing for a new challenge: summer mathematics camp all the way up in Chicago, Illinois.

My love for math had been nurtured by the close-knit relationships I had with my teachers. Ms. Juanita Turner, my Algebra II & Trigonometry teacher, had encouraged me to apply for a National Science Foundation grant to study advanced math for three weeks at Illinois Institute of Technology (I.I.T.) with about twenty-five other gifted high school juniors from all over. I was awarded the grant, which covered tuition and incidental expenses for the math camp. Ms. Turner went the extra mile and helped me make all the arrangements.

My dad drove me to the Memphis Union Train station. After saying our goodbyes, I slowly walked into the train station. I was embarking on a journey across state lines for the first time alone. Of course, I had ridden the train multiple times with my siblings to Kansas City multiple times, but never alone. The anxiety and loneliness became a running theme for the first few days of my summer camp adventure, but the trip itself was mostly uneventful.

Stepping off the train in Chicago was anything but uneventful, however. It was a surreal experience for a kid who grew up in Memphis. The skyscrapers towered overhead, slightly terrifying yet oddly alluring. The noise of the city filled my head. Even the air felt different as the Lake Michigan breeze pushed through the streets. Pedestrians appeared determined as they walked past me without a single glance. The natural energy of Chicago, the majestic skyline, the downtown area bordered on the east by Lake Michigan and the Chicago River flowing through the city boarded on both sides by high-rise condominiums as far as the eye can see, created a unique excitement for the summer to come.

Upon arriving on the IIT campus, located near 35th St. and Wabash Avenue, the first thing I noticed was that I was the only Black student. Now, let me just say I was mentally preparing myself for this exact situation, but the instinctual loneliness and apprehension were still present in my mind. How could this math camp be for all students across the whole country, and not one other Black student be present? I was somewhat unsettled by this fact. I was worried my new classmates were judging me as I was them. I later learned that one of the students had indeed been terrified he might be rooming with me, but overall, most of my math camp classmates were friendly and nerdy, like me. After the initial anxiety spike, I figured I had two options. I could walk into the camp with an undeserved inferiority complex, or I could stride into the campus with a self-assured confidence that I belonged there. I chose the latter, as the former would give me an even bigger target on my back for undesirable consequences. I was determined to do exactly what I came here for: to learn. If I made friends along the way, that would be great, but first and foremost, I was here to expand my knowledge.

Since I had never been on a college campus before, I had no knowledge of dormitory life away from home. While I am sure I could have managed, I was riddled with anxiety at the thought of sharing a room with someone who may hate me solely based on my appearance. Instead, I found myself in a single room with no roommate. The room was small and basic, furnished with just the essentials: a bed, a desk, and a sink. The bathroom and shower were in a shared common area. Meals were served at the nearby IIT cafeteria, although occasionally, I craved a hamburger from one of the fast-food places within walking distance from the campus.

Also, near campus, there was a beautiful track where I could go to work out occasionally. On one occasion, as I left campus, a man pulled up in his sedan and asked if he could give me a ride. Back home, I might have considered this offer. It wouldn't be unusual at all to be offered a ride in my own neighborhood, but this was clearly not one of my trusted neighbors, and I declined his invitation. Days later, I saw the same man in the same car, cruising slowly past groups of young students. By the third time I saw him moving slowly in his sedan, I suspected he was a pedophile or some other kind of predator, and I was sure glad I didn't climb into the car with him.

As the only Black student among a group of twenty-five, I didn't encounter any overt racism. Being part of a group of nerds, everyone tended to keep to themselves. However, I remember discussing future plans with a few students. Many expressed a strong desire to attend MIT, which aligned with my own aspirations. Little did they know, MIT was also my top choice. One student made an intriguing, slightly offensive suggestion that it might be easier for me, as a Black person, to choose any school I wanted. Mind you, this was two years before Lyndon B Johnson would sign an executive order establishing Affirmative Action as a way to "promote equal opportunity," but already people were speculating about this kind of tokenism as the Civil Rights movement worked its way into the national consciousness. Sure, it was a slightly offensive comment, but looking back on that conversation always makes me chuckle.

CHAPTER 4
ONE TENTH OF A SECOND

My ability to run track was a gift in many different ways. It gave me structure, it was a physical outlet for my intense focus and energy, and it gave me freedom. When the gun fired, and I came off those blocks, my feet were lighter than air, my soul was within and without my body, and time was a myth as I glided through the air with one target on my mind: the finish line. Running for me was less about proving myself to others and more about confirming the theory that I could get better by practicing. Of course, I wanted to win races and set records, something I was able to achieve on several occasions. However, there was a great sense of accomplishment in the discipline and craftsmanship that comes from molding your body into a tool for sport.

The other gift track provided was a higher education. Through great coaching and commitment to practicing, I became one of the top high school sprinters in the state of Tennessee and even in the nation. Then, during my senior year, as my high school education was almost complete and looking forward to starting at MIT in the fall, I competed in a track competition that changed everything. It started out like most other track meets on a clear day in March. Like nearly all my track meets, this was a segregated event with only Black student athletes. The air was crisp with the last biting chills of winter as spring slowly began to bloom. The normal crowds of family and friends from the different Black high schools all waited for the start of the 100-yard dash, always one of the most competitive, crowd-pleasing and anticipated events.

As I walked out onto the track, I felt the weight of expectations on my shoulders because I, along with my nemesis, Willie Dawson of Melrose High, had previously recorded the city's best times in the 100-yard dash. I set my feet in the starting blocks, and before the gun started, I took one last glance at my opponents on both sides of me. I had trained really hard for this race, and despite all the pressure, I felt prepared and cautiously confident. The crowd noise suddenly died down, and the air became so quiet that I could only hear my breathing. Then the starting gun went off with a loud crack, and I shot out of the blocks like a coiled spring and launched myself forward, feet flying, arms pumping, head held high.

That day, I not only set a new state record in the 100-yard dash, but I also broke Jesse Owens' national high school record of 9.4 seconds by posting a winning time of 9.3 seconds. I was officially the fastest high schooler in recorded history—in the whole nation. That one small tenth of a second changed the course of events for the rest of my life.

I received some state and national coverage for the

record-breaking run, but it was very limited. The media of the 1960s did not spend much of their precious time covering Black student-athletes or Black, segregated track meets. However, the lack of media coverage did not seem to affect the letters I received from college recruiters hoping I would become a part of their track team. The offers came pouring in from all over the nation, and several schools, including UCLA, Villanova, Southern California, and West Point, aggressively pursued me by offering recruiting trips to their institution. After my recruiting visit to West Point, I received a letter of recommendation from the then Tennessee Congressman, Dan Kuykendall, a requirement for admission to West Point.

It wasn't just track, of course. I also received academic scholarship offers and letters from schools with excellent music programs who wanted me to join their bands. As the finish line of my senior year was fast approaching, I had numerous options to consider, each one offering a different path into the future.

The Massachusetts Institute of Technology (MIT) had been my dream school for as long as I could remember, even before the days of solving equations from their monthly magazine. After years of studying and dreaming of an opportunity to one day attend this prestigious institution, I thought it would be a dream come true. When college application season had started my senior year, MIT was at the top of my list, and now I waited in anticipation for a letter in the mail, hoping and praying that I could soon consider myself a student there. After weeks of waiting patiently by the mailbox, I finally received a letter with the MIT logo on that manilla envelope.

Now a letter from anyone is important. Letters can represent a change in your life or relationships, bringing good or bad news. At the time, the letter I held in my hands felt like the most important news I had ever received. My future was a mere inches away. Sure, I had other college offers in athletics, music, and academics, but an MIT acceptance letter would be the one that I had dreamed of for four years.

I had tried to prepare for a rejection letter, just in case, but I knew I would still be devastated if that's what was in this envelope. To this day, the memory of opening that large envelope gives me goosebumps. I slowly slid the papers out and began to read. Then I read again. Then I read faster. I flipped through the pages. MIT had not only offered acceptance but a full academic scholarship. It was everything I had hoped for and more. I enthusiastically broke the news to my parents and my siblings, but they clearly were not as excited as I was. Perhaps they saw something in my future that I couldn't see yet. I'll never know. All I knew was at that moment, I was certain that I would attend MIT.

My decision at this point did not stop the influx of college recruiting letters. Our dining room table was covered with more than fifty scholarship and athletic offers from colleges and universities from all over the nation. I still remember receiving a letter from UCLA alumnus Rayford Johnson, the 1960 Olympic decathlon champion, urging me to join their program. I even received an official letter from a congressman encouraging me to consider attending West Point.

Though I was grateful for each letter I received, I could not help noticing the conspicuous lack of interest from Southeastern

Conference (SEC) schools, not even from the University of Tennessee (UT) in my home state. They were as quiet as church mice when it came to recruiting me because of my skin color. Meanwhile, I watched several top White athletes from Memphis who could not match my numbers on the track or in the classroom, secure scholarships to SEC schools. Apparently, their acceptance and scholarship criteria were based on something more than classroom performance and athletic abilities. What's more, those student-athletes who attended UT and went on to become All-Americans in their sport had a much greater likelihood of being inducted into the Tennessee Sports Hall of Fame. Even in high school, I could recognize this as yet another barrier that was placed in front of Black students. It wasn't so much about me wanting to attend UT or other SEC schools, because they were not on the top of my list. I had so many other offers from institutions that were not biased against Black student-athletes. But the realization that my race played a significant role in their decision not to recruit me was infuriating.

I believe sports serve as a microcosm of our society. The beauty of athletics is that it can break down barriers that might have otherwise kept you from accessing certain opportunities and spaces, especially if you become a well-known athlete. That said, I don't particularly like the notion that a high social status is the ticket to being treated with dignity and respect. I have always loved the quote by Muhammad Ali: "I don't trust anyone who's nice to me but rude to the waiter. Because they would treat me the same way if I were in that position." Even now, if I meet a stranger on the golf course or in a social setting, I rarely disclose that I am a physician. I don't want or need special attention or acknowledgment because of my title or profession. I used to hate it when a new patient came to my office and asked: "Do you know who I am?" As if that warrants special or immediate attention. My office staff and I took pride in rendering eye care to everyone with the same respect, dignity, and care. This included the occasional uninsured, low-income, non-English-speaking Mexican patient. Carolyn, my office manager, who is half Mexican, translated for us.

So, while I continued to consider other colleges, MIT remained my top choice, and I felt certain that was where I would be in the fall. But you just never know what's waiting for you right around the corner. During one of the final track meets of the season, an unfamiliar face appeared on the sidelines, watching me intently. Eventually, he introduced himself to my coaches, and finally, I got to learn who this mysterious stranger was. The man turned out to be Alex Wilson, the head coach of Notre Dame's track and field team. He had come all the way from Indiana to personally watch me run, to meet my parents, and to recruit me. Then, after the meet, he offered to fly me to South Bend to visit Notre Dame's campus.

For all the recruiting letters and scholarship offers I had received, I had never been wooed quite like this, and it made a strong impression. Notre Dame's campus made an even stronger impression. It was absolutely beautiful in the full bloom of late spring. The university was steeped in history and tradition. They had incredible academics that were respected the world over. And the Fighting Irish had one of the greatest athletics programs in the whole country. It was the complete package, appealing to every part of my personality, and by the time I returned home to Memphis, I was completely smitten with the idea of attending. Coach Wilson was an intelligent, soft-spoken, tea-drinking gentleman who knew all the nuances of coaching, and I believed he could mold me into a better and stronger athlete. Wilson himself was a 1928 Canadian Olympic silver medalist in the 4 X 400-meter relay.

By accepting the full athletic scholarship to Notre Dame, I also knew that I would be reducing any financial burden on my family. Everything was paid for: tuition, room and board, books, laundry, and incidentals. My older siblings were already in college. Avar was a sophomore at LeMoyne-Owen College, an HBCU in Memphis, and our dad's alma mater. Leon Jr. was then a junior at Wilberforce University in Ohio. Neither was on a full scholarship. I remember feeling it was important to reduce my parents' financial burden, and Notre Dame was the perfect school to do that while advancing as a student and developing as an athlete. I signed a letter of intent to attend Notre Dame in the fall of 1965, much to the dismay of several institutions that had heavily recruited me.

By 1965, my chapter in high school was finally over. My academic career at Manassas High overflowed with lifelong friendships, opportunities, and achievements. During my time, I won three consecutive city-wide math contests, completed four advanced placement courses, was elected senior class president, and rose to the top rank of National Defense Cadet Corps (NDCC) student battalion commander (Lt. Colonel). I even received some national media attention, alongside my first cousins, Carol and Cathryn Branham, who were not only twin sisters but the valedictorian and salutatorian of our class. Cathryn, Carol and Charles were the offspring of my dad's sister, Mrs. CharlesEtta Branham. Our stories made the cover of the popular JET magazine in April 1965.

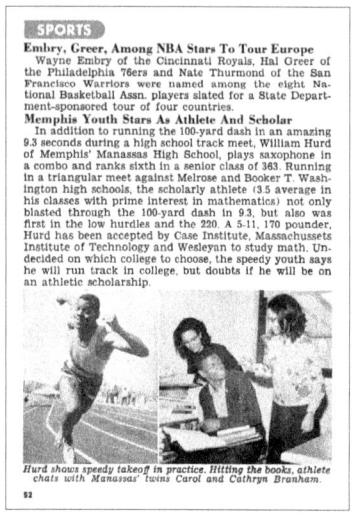

My twin cousins. Source: Jet Magazine

While my childhood and high school years at Manassas High School did not seem extraordinary to me at the time, the quality of the education and the accomplishments of my classmates have turned out to be nothing short of amazing. For example, there were several Manassas students from the 1960s era living in Scutterfield and surrounding neighborhoods like New Chicago, Klondike, and Smokey City who became physicians, dentists and attorneys. My next-door neighbor, Marvin Bledsoe, Manassas '64, practiced dentistry in Manteca, California, near the Bay area, south of Sacramento. His pediatric dental practice treated over 30,000 children over three decades before his retirement in 2010. Other medical doctors from the mid 1960's Manassas classes included Dr. Earline Houston, the first Black female graduate of the University of Tennessee College of Medicine in 1967. The Houston family lived only a few doors down from the Hurds, and her father, Earl, was a postman like my dad, Leon. She practiced psychiatry in Philadelphia up until her untimely death in 1986.

Another 1960s era Manassas High graduate was Dr. Barbara Duncan-Cody (obstetrics and gynecology). Barbara was also my classmate at Meharry Medical College class of 1980. She struggled to cope with being a victim of attrition by racism at the University of Tennessee Medical School her first year, subsequently graduating from Meharry, followed by a successful Ob-Gyn private practice. Barbara's unfortunate ordeal with the U.T. Medical School in 1975 and her eventual success as a primary health care provider demonstrates, if nothing else, how institutional racism can negatively impact a life. Later, Dr. Barbara Duncan-Cody went on to become a well-respected and successful Ob-Gyn clinician and health care provider in Memphis.

Manassas High School arguably had the most impressive compilation of jazz artists and musical icons from any high school in the nation. An incomplete list would include Isaac Hayes, Charles Lloyd (my uncle), Harold Maybern, George Coleman, Booker Little, Edward Lewis Smith, Emerson Able, Onzie Horne, Jimmy Lunceford, Sydney Kirk, Herb Smith, Frank Strozier, Andy Goodrich, and Howard Grimes. Charles Eubanks (aka Mmadu), who also grew up with me, later lived on a farm in Puerto Rico and was a multilingual musician who traveled the world.

I visited Mmadu multiple times in Puerto Rico to perform together in concerts or other musical events, and I would be the first person he called when he visited Memphis. I would listen in awe as he sang in Portuguese while playing his guitar, with me accompanying him on saxophone. Mmadu died on April 22, 2022, of kidney failure because of his unwillingness to undergo kidney dialysis, a personal choice that I understood and respected. It was hard for me to see him die when I knew that conventional medicine could have saved him. He devoted his adult life to world travel, music, and vegetarianism. We would have intense discussions about the pros and cons of traditional western medicine vs. eastern herbal therapy. I had a very deep respect for his strong convictions and understandably did not try to sway him from his beliefs. Typical of my close friends, Mmadu and I would often share constructive criticism of each other's horn playing. Before his death, I posted a rare video of me playing my flute on YouTube. Shortly afterward, Mmadu called me from Puerto Rico and said: "Man, I really liked that video of you playing alto saxophone, but Hurd, your flute playing sucks." I laughed, but I knew it was an honest evaluation from a friend and fellow musician that I would not have gotten otherwise. That constructive criticism led me to devote hours of practice time to my flute. I think of Mmadu every time I play my flute. If he could hear me now, he would be proud of my improvements.

My academic, athletic, musical, and leadership skills were all nurtured and developed at Manassas High with the help of remarkable teachers and coaches. Equally important, my penchant for hard work and practice had been ingrained into me, setting me up for future success. Those skills, along with my friendships with so many other talented students, turned out to be lifelong gifts and prepared me for the coming challenges of college.

PART II
UNIVERSITY OF NOTRE DAME

CHAPTER 5

SETTLING IN

I arrived at Notre Dame on a crisp fall day in 1965. When I first set foot on campus, I was taken in, once more, by the beauty of the place: the golf course, the ivy-covered dorms, the golden dome, the "Touchdown Jesus" library, and the picturesque, calming lakes. The actual university name is "Notre Dame du Lac," which translates to "Our Lady of the Lake." A mix of excitement and guarded anticipation filled me as I considered the challenges ahead. Despite the beauty and despite all the confidence I carried with me from my high school experience, it was still a culture shock to cross this campus, sit in an orientation hall, stand in a lunch line, or walk through the halls of my dormitory surrounded by a sea of white faces.

It's not that I lacked experience co-existing with white people; I had attended math camps and other integrated events over the years. But the vast majority of my life had been spent in a strictly segregated South. For so many years, I had been told I wasn't welcome in white schools, white swimming pools, white restaurants, white churches, white sporting events, and on and on. Now, here I was, living in a predominantly white world. I was one of nine Black freshmen out of about 1,600 entering freshmen. That means Black students made up one half of one percent (0.5%) of the class. It was simply hard to feel at home for the first few months of this new experience. Even the names were different here. At Notre Dame, guys named Robert are called Bob. Those named James are called Jim. So, after being William or William Charles all my life, now at Notre Dame, I became Bill Hurd. I was a bit unsettled in a world so far from my own; my family was miles away, and so were the familiar and friendly faces.

After navigating freshman registration and orientation, I headed to my assigned dorm room, #214, in Breen-Phillips Hall. I am not a stranger to sharing and co-habituating spaces with others, considering that I had three siblings back home. But again, it was strange for me to consider sharing a room with a White person. Mike Holtzapfel was already there, and we were both surprised to find ourselves paired together. Mike hailed from Ironton, Ohio, a small town with fewer than 10,000 residents. I began settling in with my few possessions, and Mike and I talked about how we would like to share the small space. As we spoke, a realization spread through me like a small epiphany. I suddenly realized nobody had more claim over the room than the other. Mike wasn't telling me what I was allowed to do or where to sleep. There was no "back of the bus" or "Coloreds Only" section here. Sadly, this was a legitimate shock for me. It was liberating, for sure, but also bewildering.

It was clear that Mike was just as uncomfortable as I was. He had grown up with minimal contact with Black people, and I often wondered if the Notre Dame housing board had considered this when assigning my roommate. I think it was done purposely to pair two guys from different cultures. In those first few weeks, it felt as if we were worlds apart. The way he spoke, the music he listened to, and even his style of dress felt foreign to me. His taste in music, which I perceived as nothing short of hillbilly music, baffled me. Where was the jazz, the R&B, the soul? Even with my trained musical ear, this country and folk music was not my taste. Living with someone who lacked basic relationships with Black individuals made it challenging to interpret his words and actions. I found myself questioning whether he was racist or simply unaware, grappling with my own judgments based on his background. It was a stalemate in character assessment, as I was judging him for potentially judging me.

Beyond race, our cultural differences were also pronounced, largely shaped by our backgrounds—he from southern Ohio and I from west Tennessee. These disparities often led to small hiccups. For example, Mike loved to sleep with the window open, even in the dead of winter. That was so strange to me. We were opposites in many ways, yet somewhere along the way, we began to understand each other. I'm not sure when he transitioned from being just my roommate to simply Mike. Perhaps it happened during the many hours we spent just talking and listening to music that I introduced him to over the semester. Before I knew it, Mike was grooving to the sounds of Marvin Gaye, even as he continued to sleep with the windows open. Dealing with our differences was simply a learning curve of a different kind. Mike and I grew up in two different cultural settings, and we were arbitrarily paired to share a freshman dormitory room. But in the final analysis, there was a healthy transition, starting with stereotypical preconceptions and ending with a friendship that recognized our differences but flourished with what we had in common.

There were a couple of White student-athletes from Memphis who were Notre Dame upperclassmen, but they often tried not to acknowledge me, even if our paths crossed on campus. Because I arrived as a highly recruited athlete, there was quite a bit of fanfare and public attention (not to mention expectations) around me. It seemed like there might be a degree of envy combined with discomfort coming from my fellow Caucasian Memphians.

My Black classmates, however, were wonderful to be around and quick to bond. Since there were so few of us, the nine Black freshmen quickly got to know each other. Three of us were student-athletes, including Dwight Murphy and Bob Whitmore, both basketball players. I was the only Black person on the entire track team at that time, and I felt the weight of being a representative, but I found great camaraderie in the company of these classmates. I was intrigued by the stories they told about their experiences growing up in other parts of the country, and I especially loved the stories of the students who grew up in New York City. Their tales were like something out of a novel and seemed far more interesting than anything I did in Memphis.

But if I lacked exciting stories, I excelled in other ways. I had a theory that if I put in the work and stayed confident, my preparation would stand on its own. The first proof of this theory came when I was able to skip the first semester of Calculus I. I had already done similar coursework in an Advanced Placement class I took in high school. I felt just as prepared as anyone to succeed at Notre Dame, even more prepared than some students. Coming from Manassas High School instilled a sense of pride that could not be discounted. I had rubbed elbows with some of the most intelligent and talented people to grace Memphis. I was attending Notre Dame to continue my education and be the best student and athlete that I could be. There was no urge for me to impress anyone. I was comfortable in my own skin.

People often ask me why I didn't join a Black fraternity like the Kappas or Omegas. The answer was simple. We, the Black students, were our own fraternity. During the 1960s, Notre Dame was an all-male campus with a strict curfew, which made it hard for the only nine Black freshmen to hang out much since we all lived on different parts of campus. But we made it work. We studied together, helped those who needed help, played highly competitive bid whist card games, and partied hard on weekends. There were nearby colleges between South Bend and Chicago (90 miles west of Notre Dame), like Valparaiso University and Goshen College, that bussed in Black female college students to meet and mix in the Rathskeller room of the Student Center.

My first year at Notre Dame exposed me to a diverse range of cultures, even among Black students. Many of the Black upperclassmen at Notre Dame seemed to come from well-to-do families.

There was Algernon Cooper (AJ) from Mobile, Alabama, whose family owned prominent funeral businesses. As a senior, AJ drove a very spiffy British racing green MG sports car. After graduation, he entered New York University Law School in 1966. On my first trip to New York City for a track event in the winter of 1967, AJ invited me for dinner at his apartment in Greenwich Village in Upper Manhattan. He would eventually have a successful career as an attorney and serve as the mayor of Prichard, Alabama, from 1972 to 1980.

Another notable upperclassman was Lenny Woods, who was two years my senior. Always well-dressed, soft-spoken, and generous with his knowledge and wisdom, Lenny left a lasting impression. I fondly remember our many conversations, but what stands out most is his annual return to campus each fall in a brand-new Buick Riviera. It turned out that his father owned car dealerships in the Chino Hills area near Los Angeles. During one spring break, Lenny invited me to join him and another Black upperclassman, Bill Haley from Detroit, on a road trip. We drove in his new Riviera from South Bend to Nashville, Tennessee, where we celebrated spring-break at Fisk University. It was a fun-filled and memorable trip, and at that point in my collegiate life, I had never seen such a large group of attractive women.

I made several lifelong friends during my four years at Notre Dame, though memories of three Black upperclassmen stand out to me. Frank Yates (now deceased), a junior at Notre Dame, was from Memphis and graduated from Father Bertrand High School. Frank was always there for me to lend his support and encouragement.

He later became a mentor to me and donated his notes from differential equations and physics courses. Yates finished his college career with a near-perfect GPA and was selected as a Fulbright Scholar. He received his PhD in statistical psychology from the University of Michigan and eventually became a tenured professor there. Another friend was Ron Homer, initially a pre-med student who later switched to business and grew up in Brooklyn, New York. He was an easy-going guy who maintained a level head, even in the most difficult situations. This was something I always admired about him as he seemed very cool to most people. He was one of those New Yorkers who seemed to have all the answers.

Dick Arlington, an All-American in football and wrestling, became a good friend. And then there was Alan Page, an All-American defensive end at Notre Dame. Alan went on to NFL stardom and the NFL Hall of Fame after playing with the Minnesota Vikings as one of the "Purple People Eaters." After law school, he became the Honorable Alan Page, the first Black Minnesota Supreme Court Justice. At Notre Dame, he was one of the first notable Black athletes to sport a shaved head. Handy with a pair of clippers, he became my designated barber, too.

My own Notre Dame athletic career started with great expectations. When I arrived on campus in 1965, the NCAA restricted freshmen from competing in NCAA sports competitions. However, there were other options to compete. To keep my motor running, so to speak, coach Alex Wilson entered me into a series of high-profile national and international invitational track meets that took me all over the world.

One of these events was the Millrose Games in Madison Square Garden. This was my first trip to New York City, and I was excited to compete at the collegiate level and to visit this place I had heard so much about. After winning my semifinal heat of the 60-yard dash, I took the short walk back to my nearby hotel and discovered a package waiting for me at the front desk. When I got to my room and opened the package, there were three crisp $100 bills and a pair of gold and very light-weight Puma sprinting shoes. In those days, Puma made arguably the finest track shoes in the country, so this was a very kind gift. So I thought. They were even tinted light gold to match Notre Dame's team colors. The accompanying note explained that the shoes were a gift from the company itself but did not mention where the financial contribution came from.

This kind of thing turned out to be rather commonplace over the years, as athletic companies provided gear and Notre Dame boosters and organizers would provide small donations, plane tickets, or other support for traveling athletes. Keep in mind that in 1965, I was still considered an amateur athlete by NCAA standards.

I wore those gold Pumas in the 60-yard dash finals and ended up coming in second place, just behind Charlie Green from the University of Nebraska. I was disappointed not to win, but I couldn't feel too bad about it since this was the same Charlie Green who would win a gold medal in the 4x100-meter relay and a silver medal in the open 100 meters a few years later in the 1968 Mexico City Olympic games.

After my races, excited to see the city, I strolled around Manhattan. I was in awe of the city and marveled at the hustle and bustle. Walking the streets of Memphis, you were almost sure to be on the receiving end of some southern hospitality, but in New York, no one—White, Black, Asian, Latino, mixed, or other—spared me a second glance. That is until I ran into Willadene Ingram near 34th Street and 7th Avenue.

Willadene Ingram was one of my high school classmates from Manassas who now lived in Manhattan. We were both shocked and delighted to run into each other right in the middle of a busy New York sidewalk. We ducked into a local coffee shop to have a quick chat, and I explained my trip to New York. Willadene, in perfect New York fashion, was quickly back out the door as she rushed to an appointment. When I returned to Notre Dame, I told several of my track mates about the chance encounter, and they simply wouldn't believe me. It was basically the same odds as winning the lottery.

Despite their lack of faith in my travel stories, my Notre Dame track teammates were great. We trained hard together and had fun getting to know each other during our daily practices. I often worried about my teammates' perception of me since I was the focus of so much publicity and press coverage. Despite this, I never felt any negativity from my teammates in the form of envy, jealousy, or racism. This felt especially valuable to me since I was the only Black person on the team. I wanted to cultivate a relationship with them based on sportsmanship and the brotherhood that comes with this.

CHAPTER 6
SHENANIGANS

During my sophomore year, on a chilly Saturday morning, November 19, 1966, I participated in an event that many people considered crazy, but for us, was a fun adventure. Starting at the fifty-yard line of Notre Dame Stadium, a relay team of enthusiastic students and athletes took off on a nonstop 158-mile run to East Lansing, Michigan. A good crowd of students and faculty had gathered to send us off, and we waved as we crossed campus and headed out onto the roadways.

Just a week before, the Irish football team had delivered a blowout win over Duke, 64-0, and now the stage was set for the 1966 national championship. Undefeated and top-rated, Notre Dame was set to face off against the also undefeated Michigan State University in East Lansing. After fifty years, some of the details have faded from my memory, but one thing remains clear: the sheer audacity of the idea. This event became known as the 1966 Notre Dame Sophomore Relay Run to Spartan

Stadium. The plan was simple yet ambitious. Taking turns running one mile at a time, we would relay a football all the way to Spartan Stadium.

As the idea spread through the university, it picked up momentum, and soon, numerous students and faculty wanted to contribute. What began as a small group quickly grew to twenty-five participants. To accommodate everyone and our supplies, we decided to rent a bus. Among us were my track teammates, Ed Broderick, a high jumper, and Joe Quigley, a half-miler, along with cross-country team members Dan Saracino and Mark Walsh. Although not able to join us, classmates Mike Maloy and Dennis Nigro played key roles as co-chairmen, handling planning and logistics. We were fortunate that most of our needs—like football jerseys and equipment—were donated. The North Dining Hall provided us with box lunches, and the student body raised funds to help cover the cost of the shuttle bus.

On Friday afternoon, the day before the big game, we loaded onto the shuttle bus and set off on our adventurous relay run from South Bend to East Lansing, covering a total of 158 miles. Fueled by adrenaline and the pure hilarity of the event, we had a good time. The harsh weather turned out to be the greatest challenge, and I vividly remember being pelted by cold November rain as I ran one of my night legs, but the camaraderie among us made it all worthwhile. Our adventure even made the pages of the November 17, 1966, edition of The Observer Group, where it was featured on page four, complete with photographs documenting our journey.

The 1966 Notre Dame Sophomore Relay Run to Spartan Stadium

Source: The Observer

Ironically, despite the effort we put into this relay, none of us had tickets to the game. Fortunately, the Notre Dame basketball coach, Johnny Dee, learned about our relay run and ticket predicament. Using his connections and reputation, he worked with the MSU athletic director to secure us access to the game. The matchup ended in a 10-10 tie, but Notre Dame was awarded the 1966 national championship due to our pregame number-one ranking.

Back at Notre Dame, I was starting to feel a little bit like a star athlete myself as groups of people began gathering near the finish line of the 60-yard dash to cheer me on at many of the home track meets in the Joyce Center. I would see many of my fellow Black Notre Dame students and local people from South Bend gathered there, and it was exciting to see a crowd of mostly

Black spectators cheering. As the only Black member of the track team, being surrounded by that enthusiasm was meaningful.

Winning the 60-yard dash at Notre Dame

Despite our differences in political ideology and cultural backgrounds, my track teammates were always respectful and supportive. By my junior year, I was elected team captain, and I shared many fun and playful moments with teammates like Ole Skarstein, Bob Timm, Pete Farrell, Ken Howard, Jack Samar and Mark Walsh, who made bus trips and practices fun and joyful.

In 1965, Ole Skarstein arrived at Notre Dame as the national Norwegian 100-meter champion. As freshmen, we became friends and have remained so ever since. Ole, an architecture major with a passion for photography, set up a small darkroom in his dormitory for developing film. Some of his photographs are included in this memoir. Much later in life, during the summer of 2008, Ole, then a retired architect living in Bodø, Norway, graciously hosted four Notre Dame track teammates, including myself. The group—Bob Walsh, Dr. Mark Walsh, Dr. Doug Brenlin, and me—traveled from Chicago to Oslo and then to Bodø. Ole provided us with a memorable Norwegian experience, including salmon fishing, boat rides, hiking, and golfing in the midnight sun.

From L-R Our Norwegian host, Ole Skarstein, me, Dr. Doug Brenlin, Dr. Mark Walsh, Bob Walsh

In April 2017, Ole's daughters gave him a trip to America for his 70th birthday, with specific stops in Nashville, Memphis, and New Orleans. As the designated tour guide for Memphis, I aimed to show Ole and his daughters the best of what the city had to offer. We visited the Memphis Pyramid (now home to Bass Pro Shops), the FedEx Forum, and the National Civil Rights Museum.

We enjoyed famous Memphis barbecue ribs, strolled down Beale Street, and, at Ole's daughters' request, toured Graceland, Elvis Presley's historic home. I explained to them why, like many Black Memphians I know, I had not visited Graceland myself—not out of disrespect for Elvis's achievements but due to a personal lack of interest. Instead, I highlighted other aspects of Memphis's rich musical heritage, including artists like Isaac Hayes, and took them on a tour of north Memphis, where I grew up. Overall, I believe they had a great time.

At Notre Dame, it was uncommon for sprinters, hurdlers, and jumpers to hang out with distance and cross-country runners. Mark Walsh and I—a distance runner and a sprinter—formed a close friendship that continues to this day. On one memorable bus trip, we played Hearts the entire way. Ole, an accomplished photographer with a darkroom in his dorm, would take candid shots of his teammates. I still have some playful photos of Bob Timm and me coming out of the shower after practice, taken by Ole. Mark often jokes that I once said it was the first time I had taken a shower with a White man.

Meanwhile, Rhynette and I did a good job of staying in touch. As teenagers, neither of us had ventured far from home, so when it was time for me to leave Memphis for Notre Dame, we both believed we could maintain a close relationship. Two years later, Rhynette enrolled at Mount Holyoke College in South Hadley, Massachusetts. Our college experiences mirrored those of many students as we enjoyed the excitement of meeting new and interesting people. Yet, we managed to keep our romantic relationship alive. We wrote long letters to each other often and managed the occasional phone call. Rhynette visited me a few times over the years, and I made it to Mt. Holyoke once too. Despite the fact that the athletics department was flying me all over the country for track events, it was still pretty difficult for us to travel personally, and our two schools were separated by 814 miles and five states. But that didn't stop us from trying.

On one occasion, Rhynette surprised me by showing up at a track meet at Bowling Green State University in Ohio. That's when she won the hearts of my coach and teammates, too; they recognized what an effort she made to be there. On another occasion, Rhynette hitched rides all the way to see me. Combining ride shares and hitchhiking, she made it all the way to Notre Dame. In today's world, hitchhiking is much more risky and perhaps ill-advised. Nevertheless, I was genuinely touched that she would go to such lengths to see me. Of course, we still had those strict curfews and visiting hours to work around. Female guests were only allowed on campus briefly during weekends, so Rhynette would stay with our friends, Arl and Teresa Williams, who lived just two blocks away from campus but were also from Memphis. Those visits became precious moments for us, and I cherished every one of them.

Arl, who was enrolled in the Notre Dame Law School, graduated the same year I did, in 1969. Years later, he would become the director of human resources at Dulles Airport in Washington, D.C. Standing a towering 6'2", Arl always took great care in his appearance, looking impeccably dressed every time I saw him. Back in high school, he played quarterback for Father Bertrand High in

Memphis, dominating the field with both passion and a well-built physique.

Tragically, later in life, Arl fell ill with pancreatic cancer, which resulted in him losing most of his body mass. During a trip to Washington, D.C., to support my brother Leon during his open-heart surgery, I took the opportunity to visit Arl and Teresa. I was shocked by how much weight he had lost; he had shrunk to the point where none of his clothes fit him anymore. His closet was filled with Armani pants, sports jackets, cashmere sweaters, and matching tracksuits, all now too large for him.

To my surprise, Arl insisted that I take his clothes. Initially, I hesitated, unsure about accepting such a generous gesture, but I realized they would likely end up at Goodwill otherwise. Eventually, I packed up all his belongings and shipped them back to Memphis, where I planned to have the items tailored. To this day, Arl's clothes are staples of my wardrobe. He lives on through these pieces, and I find myself in a constant state of fond memories whenever I wear them.

Reflecting on these connections—Rhynette's unwavering support and Arl's generous spirit—I realize how deeply intertwined our lives became, each moment a reminder of the bonds we forged during those formative years.

Another person who supported me wonderfully was my father. Usually, his love and pride were steady and measured, something I always felt and held close. But occasionally, he would still surprise me. In 1967, when I was a junior at Notre Dame, my dad bought me a 1964 Mustang, silver with a red interior and an 8-track player. I was astonished. It was the most wonderful—and expensive—gift that I had ever received from anyone. I still don't know how he pulled that off on a postal worker's salary while also supporting my two older siblings with their college tuition. But he did it.

    I couldn't wait to take Rhynette for a spin.

CHAPTER 7
THE NEED FOR SPEED

In 1967, not only was I the proud new owner of a silver Ford Mustang, but I competed in the Central Collegiate Conference (CCC) indoor track meet, which inspired me to reach new heights. I settled into the blocks next to Loyola University's George Crosby, who had just set an American record in the indoor 300-yard dash. I had been looking forward to competing against him for weeks now. The gun went off, the sprinters shot forward, and, once more, the whole universe seemed to slow down and concentrate itself around the seconds it took to blaze across the straightaway, fly into the last turn, and reach that finish line. Despite all my efforts and anticipation, I came in second place.

Some defeats sting worse than others, and that particular experience lingered in my mind for a full year as I prepared to face him again. The much taller George Crosby became my nemesis in that race, and I was determined to reclaim my position. I thought about it during training and conditioning. I thought about it during other competitions and while I was implementing new sprinting techniques. I couldn't wait to face him again.

I had other challenges to overcome. In the spring of that same year, the team was traveling by bus from South Bend, Indiana, to Williamsburg, Virginia, where the College of William and Mary hosted the William & Mary Relays every year. To break up the long bus ride, we opted to stop at a small motel in rural Virginia. After so many hours, we piled out of the bus and gazed upon the white building with green shutters and a backdrop of trees thick with new leaves. We could practically feel the comfortable beds from here in the parking lot. Even the mowed grass looked comfortable enough to sleep on. But then we got inside.

All fifteen of us gathered in the small lobby as Coach Wilson engaged the desk clerk. The clerk's eyes scanned our faces, but his gaze lingered on me, the only Black person here. In a sea of 15 white faces, I stood out like a duck amongst swans, and I could immediately sense his antipathy. I refused to look away from the clerk. I might be denied a room, but I wasn't going to be meek for this man. Although the moment lasted only a few seconds, it felt interminable, with his blue eyes locked on my brown ones. After a tense silence, the motel clerk announced, "The Negro can't stay here."

Coach Wilson calmly but immediately replied, "If he can't stay, then no one will."

At that moment, my teammates and Coach Wilson resembled my family as they challenged racism despite their exhaustion after a long day. The team grabbed their bags and exited the premises. Eventually, we found a more hospitable hotel.

Almost a year later, on March 23, 1968, I finally got my chance to race Loyola University's George Crosby again. At the Western Michigan Relays in Kalamazoo, Michigan, we met once more on the track, and I was thrilled. While George was 6'2" and more of a quarter-miler, I was a sprinter at heart, and I hoped I could turn that to my advantage. We settled into our starting blocks, placed at intervals. The staggered lanes ensured that the runner in the farthest outside lane would cover the same distance as the runner in the inside lane. I was in lane 4, with George in lane 5, meaning I started off looking at his back, hungry to make up that distance.

When the starting gun fired, I surged forward, quickly making up the distance around the first turn. I had trained hard and was fully prepared, fueled by the memory of that previous year's race. I knew that if we emerged from the last turn, neck and neck, my closing speed would give me the edge I needed. Sure enough, when we came out of the last turn, we were right beside each other. That's when I gave it everything I had. All the training, all the focus, all the preparation came down to these final seconds of the race.

Not only did I win the race, but I also set a new American record of 29.8 seconds in the indoor 300—a record that would stand for two years. George was gracious in defeat, congratulating me after I broke his record. That same day at the Western Michigan meet, I also shattered the Fieldhouse record with a time of 6.0 seconds in the 60-yard dash.

BILL HURD
American Indoor Record Holder

BILL HURD

On March 23, 1968, Notre Dame's Bill Hurd flashed across the finish line in the Western Michigan Relays' 300-yard dash in the American Indoor record time of :29.8 besting what was probably the nation's finest assemblage of 300-yard sprinters. At Kalamazoo, Hurd clipped two-tenths of a second off the previous mark.

For the junior from Memphis, Tenn., the :29.8 clocking in the 300 is only one of many performances that rate him Notre Dame's hallmark sprinter.

Hurd enrolled at Notre Dame in September of 1965 as a highly touted prep athlete credited with a wind-aided :09.3 100-yard performance at Manassas High in Memphis. As a freshman, Hurd finished second to George Anderson, National AAU 100-meter champ, in the Michigan AAU Meet's 60-yard dash in :06.1 and two weeks later claimed a victory in the 60 yard dash at the Michigan Federation Meet at Kalamazoo establishing new meet, fieldhouse, and Notre Dame freshman records with a :06.0 clocking. At the National Federation Championships in New York, Hurd placed second behind three-time NCAA champion Charlie Greene in :06.2.

Hurd's best cinder performance came in his debut at the Kentucky Relays when he set a meet record in the 100-yard dash qualifying event with a :09.5 only to place second in the same time in the finals.

Hurd began this year by asking Coach Ara Parseghian for a trial period with the Fighting Irish football team—an interesting request considering he hadn't played football in high school.

Hurd was a superb indoor performer in 1968 copping first-place awards in his first five of six 60-yard dash starts. At the IC4A Meet in New York, Hurd captured the 60-yard title with a :06.2 clocking.

In addition to his track efforts, Hurd is a gifted musician. As a freshman, Hurd was named the "Outstanding Young Performer" in Notre Dame's Collegiate Jazz Festival and was awarded a summer scholarship to the Music Conservatory at the California campus at Berkeley.

A Dean's List student since his first semester at Notre Dame, Hurd is majoring in engineering at the University with a 3.4 grade average.

Source: Observer

It wasn't all about winning, of course. Amazing, lifelong friendships formed during these events, too. I was fortunate to meet and compete with Jim Green, an amazing sprinter and human being who was the very first Black scholarship student-athlete at the University of Kentucky. He beat me at the 1968 NCAA Indoor Track & Field championship to become the Indoor 60-yard dash champion. The event was held at Detroit's Cobo Hall, and I finished fourth in the final (followed by O.J. Simpson, who finished fifth). Jim and I became friends and would often room together on road trips to invitational track meets. In 1971, he was also the first Black student-athlete to graduate from the University of Kentucky, and he was recently honored by the university as it unveiled the new Jim Green Indoor Track and Field Center and a statue of his likeness. I surprised Jim by attending this special dedication. He and I remain close friends to this day.

The Notre Dame team participated in some very prestigious track meets. Among them were the Penn Relays, held annually in early spring at Franklin Field in Philadelphia, but, more often, the Drake Relays at Drake University Stadium in Des Moines, Iowa. In mid-April 1969, on a sunny, clear day in Des Moines, I was part of the Notre Dame Sprint Medley Relay team, which included Ole Skarstein, Doug Breunlin, Joe Quigley, and me. We weren't favored to win; many attendees and sports commentators were leaning toward the University of Kansas (KU), whose anchor leg would be run by the legendary Jim Ryun. But we were feeling good.

When the gun sounded to start the race, Ole took off as our lead runner, completing the first 220-yard leg and giving us a slight lead. I ran the second 220-yard leg, extending our lead a little further. Doug then took the baton for the 440-yard third leg, running an impressive split time of 46.0 flat. We were feeling confident. Jim Ryun was KU's ace, but we had our own secret weapon: Joe Quigley, an All-American half-miler from New York City. When the baton landed in his hand, he had a lead and a mission: don't get caught. He ran like his life depended on it, streaking across the finish line while we cheered him on madly.

To our astonishment, we not only won the race but also set a new world record in the sprint medley. When they announced our time, it was the fastest that had ever been recorded. Ever. Anywhere in the world. We were ecstatic, but our joy was short-lived. One of the event judges claimed that Ole had stepped on the inside line of his lane four times while rounding the turn. We were disqualified, and there was no way to contest the decision. Instant replay did not exist in those days, and Coach Wilson had no grounds to challenge the judge's ruling otherwise.

Track is a sport of seconds and more recently, hundredths of seconds. These fractions of seconds can be the most thrilling ones imaginable or the most crushing. One second, we were champions and world record holders. The next, we were not. While I accepted the decision, the disappointment weighed heavily on our team. Accomplishing something as monumental as a world record was incredible, and for those brief moments when we held the title, I had never felt prouder or more assured of my track teammates.

At the start of my junior year season, I had been elected team captain, and I wore that honor with pride, even when difficult circumstances arose. In 1969, the Notre Dame track team set out, once again, on the annual bus journey to Williamsburg, Virginia, for the Colonial Relay at the College of William & Mary. The bus ride was exhausting, yet the late April air was filled with a sense of anticipation. We joked and laughed, trying to shake off the weariness of the long trip.

However, our excitement quickly faded when we arrived at our accommodations. We were led to a dimly lit dormitory basement that felt more like a forgotten dungeon than a place for athletes. Bunk beds lined the cramped space, and the bathrooms and showers were barely adequate. It was as if we had been transported back to some medieval castle, prisoners of our own circumstances.

As the conditions sank in, discontent grew among my teammates. Some suggested we vote to withdraw from the Colonial Relay and head back to Notre Dame. I felt the weight of being team captain at that moment. I knew I was standing against the tide, but I couldn't shake the feeling that we were here to represent our school, and we couldn't just walk away. We had to rise above the challenges and not give in to them. When I began to speak as team captain, the dimly lit room got quiet. At this moment, I could feel the respect and the anticipation of me telling my teammates not to give up.

I expressed this to the team, and after some discussion, we agreed to stay if we could improve our accommodations. Coach Wilson took our concerns seriously. He advocated for us, reaching out to the right people at William & Mary. Thanks to his persistence, we were eventually moved to a more suitable place to rest our heads.

Once settled, we turned our focus to the competition. The atmosphere at the Colonial Relay was electric, with twelve teams vying for victory. I remember feeling a mix of nerves and excitement as we prepared to race. When it was all said and done, Notre Dame finished first in the team competition. I was awarded the

MVP honor, receiving a pocket gold watch that I still cherish to this day. I felt proud not just of our victorious performance but of the team we had become.

Receiving the 1968 Colonial Relays MVP Gold Watch

CHAPTER 8
FOOTBALL AND MUSIC

One evening, during a spring training workout in the Athletic and Convocation Center (ACC), where the track team and the football team train and work out in close proximity, the Notre Dame football coach, Ara Parseghian, walked toward me. After introducing himself to me, as if I did not already know who he was, he asked me if I would like to be a part of the Notre Dame football team. Without hesitation, I said yes.

Although football had always intrigued me, I had never played it before, and here I was, a college junior looking to pick it up for the first time. However, I had resolved not to leave Notre Dame with any regrets. I wanted to take advantage of every opportunity that came my way. I hadn't played high school football because my dad was concerned about my safety. As the city's fastest athlete, he worried that an opposing team might possess a cruel intention to break one of my legs. I always thought that if I had played high school football, I might have been a wide receiver to be reckoned with, though.

Like my dad, Coach Wilson was apprehensive about the risk of injury right before the start of the 1967 indoor track season. He wasn't thrilled that one of his most valuable track stars was going to risk his health to be a backup wide receiver, but how could I turn down the chance to join such a legendary program? The Fighting Irish football team was one of the most historic, successful, and famous teams in the world. And they had just been crowned the 1966 NCAA football national champions. And next fall, when I returned to campus, I would be a part of it.

Football players reported back to campus early to practice before the school year started. On my first day, it was clear that I didn't fit the traditional football player mold. Years of track had left me on the slimmer side, with less muscle definition than my new teammates. Many guys on the football team were 6'4" and 225 pounds, while I stood just under six feet and weighed barely 180 pounds. Before we even reached the practice field, I had to learn how to put on football pads and related gear. I also had to adjust to getting hit while protecting myself from injury.

As a track athlete, I was used to long, physically demanding practice sessions. What was new to me was the hard physical contact that the football practice sessions brought. During practice, Coach Parseghian directed the offense and defense from a high scaffold. It seemed like someone would get hurt every day, but this never stopped or even slowed down the practice sessions. The injured player was simply moved off or carted off to be cared for and everyone else carried on. I suddenly had a greater appreciation for why my track coaches weren't too pleased with my decision to play football.

My main advantage, of course, was my speed, which earned me a wide receiver position where I played second string behind the starting wide receiver and All-American Jim Seymour. I felt a bit isolated on the football team, though, as I had no prior experience and limited opportunities to form meaningful friendships with my football teammates. Additionally, I was the only Black player on the team. During preseason training camp, I was assigned a dormitory room with a tight end named Dewey Poskon, who stood 6'5" and weighed 230 pounds. We exchanged stories about our upbringing and cultural differences. We became friendly, but we were in different position groups during practice, and he had more established friendships elsewhere on the team. And then there was Coach Parseghian. Though he had recruited me, I didn't develop a personal relationship with him. He seemed almost God-like up on his scaffold or barking orders on the sidelines, commanding a reverence that made me nervous to approach him one-on-one.

Since I was the fastest person on the team, the defensive backs made sure I was aware of their daunting presence with chips and bumps as I ran past them on my wide receiver routes. Once, during practice, I caught a bullet of a pass from Terry Hanratty that came into my hands with such high velocity and with such a tight spiral that the laces on the football made a one-inch laceration on the second finger of my right hand. It was a beautiful twenty-yard gain, but I was looking down at exposed tendons and bone. I was rushed to the Notre Dame infirmary, where the finger was stitched up. Though I rarely see him, on any occasion that Terry and I cross paths, we joke about the scar he gave me. I still wear it with pride.

On September 23, 1967, I got into my first game, and the memories are still vivid. Cloudy and 67 degrees outside. We played at home against the Golden Bears from the University of California-Berkeley. We ran out of the tunnel and into a stadium filled to capacity. We were coming off the National Championship season, and there was a lot of energy in the air. We had returning players such as Rocky Bleier, who went on to play for the Pittsburgh Steelers (and was included in their Hall of Honor), was drafted by the U.S. Army during the Vietnam War, and was awarded the Bronze Star and a Purple Heart for his military service. We had Terry Hanratty, who also went on to play with the Pittsburgh Steelers, and consensus All-American wide receiver Jim Seymour, who went on to be the tenth overall pick in the 1969 NFL/AFL Draft for the Los Angeles Rams.

We built up a lead against the Golden Bears, and Coach Parseghian played a number of reserved players like myself. In some ways, it was similar to track: poised along the line of scrimmage, waiting to be released by the signal, and then shooting forward at full speed. But in most ways, this was a completely different experience, with the roar of the stadium, the gleaming helmets and pads ready to make hard contact, and the players flying at each other. I caught two passes in that game, and we won with a final score of 41–8.

Soon, however, I found myself at a crossroads. While there were still several weeks left of football, including the college bowl season, training was already beginning for the upcoming indoor track season. I had thoroughly enjoyed being a small part of Notre

Dame's storied football legacy. I loved tapping the "Play Like a Champion" sign and running through the tunnel out onto the field in front of 70,000 fans. It had been an incredibly memorable experience being on the football team, but I made the difficult decision to leave before the end of the season to rejoin my track team. I approached Coach Parseghian to thank him for the opportunity to be part of the '67 football team.

Then, I approached Coach Wilson, who was extremely pleased with this decision.

Balancing a social life with academic and athletic responsibilities proved to be an enjoyable challenge too. I eagerly embraced the feeling of independence and self-reliance, and I believed that developing as a serious musician was just as important as excelling academically and athletically.

I dedicated much of my free time to practicing my saxophone, and I played in three different student bands. The first was an R&B instrumental band, The Magnificent 7, featuring the band leader and trombonist John Buchanan from Washington, D.C. (a close friend to this day) and Oran (OJ) Johnson, a singer and multi-instrumentalist. The band was managed by Joyce Bizot, wife of Notre Dame English professor Richard Bizot. Joyce was the Founding Director of The Great American Jazz Piano Competition. Playing in the Magnificent 7 allowed undergrads a chance to have fun and make extra money.

I later joined the Notre Dame Lettermen, a big band jazz group. The Jazz Sextet and the Lettermen frequently performed at the highly acclaimed Notre Dame Collegiate Jazz Festival. Richard

Bizot, Joyce's husband, played a key role in establishing the ND CJF. In 1966, I was honored with the Miscellaneous Instrument Award for my performance on soprano saxophone. The following year, I won the Outstanding Saxophone Soloist Award at the 1967 Notre Dame Collegiate Jazz Festival. One of the judges at that event was the late Andy Goodrich, a former band director from Memphis and a fellow Manassas High alum. At that time, Goodrich was the Director of Jazz Studies at Michigan State University.

CHAPTER 9

SOCIAL LIFE, SOCIAL ISSUES, & OLYMPICS

I was often treated like royalty, being a star athlete in a school where star athletes were worshiped. Guys like Austin Carr, Rocky Bleier, Bob Whitmore, Terry Hanratty, Jim Seymour, and Alan Page, just to name a few, seemed to have a social status all to themselves. Notre Dame did not become co-ed until after I left, but St. Mary's College, located adjacent to the Notre Dame campus, provided opportunities to meet girls for those inclined. Some friends and teammates tried unsuccessfully to set me up on blind dates with girls from St. Mary's who wanted dates with star athletes. I was never comfortable with the thought of dating White girls or even crazier, girls who preferred athletes. After so many years in a strictly segregated society in Memphis, I just couldn't shake the apprehension about interracial dating. While college life was far more liberated than my hometown experiences, there was still much resistance. For example, the basketball coach forbade his own Black players from dating white women from St. Mary's. Besides all that, I still had a wonderful thing going on with Rhynette, and I felt that by not dating, I would have more time to focus on my studies, track & field, and music. I would be lying if I said all that attention wasn't a huge ego boost for me, though. It certainly was.

I had to manage my time carefully to keep up with all my goals. Staying focused on what mattered most allowed me to navigate these commitments, though it meant sacrificing some social events. There were many nights I missed out on playing bid whist with the guys or attending parties at nearby colleges with other Black students.

When I first entered Notre Dame, I began as a math major but later switched to electrical engineering, opting for an applied rather than a theoretical curriculum. As a member of the Eta Kappa Nu engineering honor society, I worked closely with study partners like Patrick Christiansen and Terrance Cahill. The classroom was actually the easiest part of my Notre Dame experience, and I credit this to the teachers at Manassas High School, where I received excellent teaching and had access to a wealth of Advanced Placement courses. By the time I arrived at Notre Dame, I had already developed strong study habits, the ability to focus, and a deep appetite for learning. This quest for knowledge continued to drive me through medical school a decade later.

Being one of only nine entering Black freshmen in 1965, I encountered plenty of social challenges, especially during the height of the racial volatility of the 1960s. As a freshman, I was the sole Black student in all my first-semester classes, and I found the experience eye-opening but not overwhelming. Soon, I received tremendous support from my track teammates also, such as Mark Walsh, Tom Buckley, and Ole Skarstein. To help matters even more, Dr. Roland Chamblee, a South Bend family physician, kindly invited me to his home for dinner with his family. Dr. Chamblee was president of the local NAACP, head of a medical clinic for the poor and uninsured, and graduated from Meharry in 1953. He reached out to me and other Black students and student-athletes. His hospitality made me feel welcome, and he even took me golfing at the nine-hole Burke Golf Course on campus. During this time, I also formed a friendship with his daughter, Sandy, which blossomed into a mutual attraction. Sandy and I remain friends to the present.

On December 7, 1968, the Notre Dame campus was covered with three inches of snow when the number one nationally ranked UCLA basketball team, coached by the legendary John Wooden, was in town with their All-American center Lew Alcindor, who would later change his name to Kareem Abdul-Jabaar. UCLA won the game 88-75, but the Black UCLA players, including Kareem, Curtis Rowe, and Sidney Wicks, accepted an invitation by the Notre Dame Black students to attend a welcome party. I will never forget seeing Kareem Abdul-Jabbar for the first time. He stood 7 feet 2 inches tall, towering above even the tallest Notre Dame basketball players, like Bob Whitmore, in the room. I remember watching him duck beneath the door ledge to fit inside. I had never seen any human being that tall before in my life. Despite his towering height, Kareem came across as a soft-spoken introvert. I remember finding this surprising. So many star athletes seemed to have big personalities to match their social status, but here was another star athlete displaying a more reserved and introverted persona, more like myself. Coincidentally, our paths would cross again exactly twenty-five years later in the spring of 1994 when Kareem and I, along with Calvin Hill (Yale), Leroy Keyes (Purdue), Jim Ryun (Kansas), and Lee Evans (San Jose State), received the 1994 NCAA Silver Anniversary Award in San Antonio, Texas.

The 1960s were a turbulent time for racial and social justice, a period when many marginalized people began to demand freedom, security, and the right to thrive. It was impossible to turn on the news without witnessing protests—whether for civil rights or against the Vietnam War. The television broadcast the suffering of people across the globe, leaving those concerned with a heavy heart. Despite the violence that too often erupted against peaceful protests, there was a sense of progress. With leaders like Martin Luther King Jr. and Malcolm X guiding the way, it felt like civil rights were gaining ground, and the dream of equality was within reach for many people of color.

But that optimism shattered on April 4, 1968, when Dr. King was assassinated, leaving a deep scar on every Black American. The news of his death echoed through every TV and radio across the nation. I was still in school when I heard the tragic announcement. For me, the pain was even more profound when I learned that King was killed in my own hometown of

Memphis, just a few miles from where I lived. A palpable dread settled over the country as if the hope of the civil rights movement had shattered into a million pieces. People hesitated to ask, "What do we do now?" Fear of the answer loomed large. Dr. King had been a guiding light, and without him, the future felt bleak and uncertain.

As a child, I had been forced to drink from "coloreds only" water fountains and sit at the back of the bus. I was fascinated by the civil rights movement, dreaming of a day when those signs would be gone. I longed for the moment when anyone could sit wherever they wanted. I longed for a time when there would be equal opportunity for people who looked like me. I dream of a scenario where your neighbor is not judged by culture, religion or skin color, but instead by how well your brain functions and how big your heart is. Dr. King's movement opened doors for people like me, and his death forced me to confront my own struggles with racism. I wondered where my own quest for equality would lead me—toward a tragic end or a brighter future. I began to think more seriously about my role on campus and how I might help make a difference for the University and future Black students.

Another conscientious student was Arthur (Art) McFarland. Although a year behind me, Art and I hit it off so well that we became dorm roommates in both my junior and senior years, and we're still close friends to the present. We lived in Alumni Hall in a large corner room with a private bath and shower, which, at that time, was rare for a Notre Dame campus dormitory. Fellow students would ask Art how on earth he got to live in such a nice dorm room. Art would proudly say to them, "Have you met my friend, Bill? He's the fastest man in America." This was around the time of my record-breaking sprints.

Art was the founder of the first Afro-American Society at Notre Dame, organized to promote Black students' interests. One of the Society's first events was a controversial protest in Washington Hall on campus, where U.S. Senator Strom Thurmond was scheduled to speak. Senator Thurmond of South Carolina was a strong advocate of racial segregation and a strong opponent of both the Civil Rights Act of 1964 and the Voting Rights Act of 1965. About twenty Black students, led by Art McFarland and including me, gathered and sat in the front row. Just as Senator Thurmond was about to start speaking, we all stood up and walked out in protest of his racist ideology. Notably, none of the Black basketball players attended the protest after their coach forbade them to participate in controversial protests. This was the same coach who told them they weren't allowed to date white women from St. Mary's College. While the protest was small in the greater scheme of history, it had an impact on campus, drawing both praise and condemnation—but sparking an important conversation that carried on in the classrooms and beyond.

Afro-American Society protests Sen. Thurmond's 1968 ND visit

Around this time, Dick Gregory emerged as a significant figure in U.S. culture. He was a comedian, actor, writer, activist, and social critic. He entered the 1968 presidential campaign, though mainstream media often dismissed him as an entertaining sideshow. His brother, Ron Gregory, was a Notre Dame graduate and an All-American half-miler.

During Dick Gregory's campaign, novelty dollar bills featuring his image and the caption "Dick Gregory for President" began to circulate. They resembled real currency in size and texture. Ron gave me a stack of these bills to promote his brother's campaign. To my surprise, I discovered that these Gregory bills worked like the real deal when inserted into a dollar-changing machine, producing quarters just like genuine money.

One evening during the 1968 indoor track meet season, half of the Notre Dame track team traveled to Cleveland, Ohio, for the Knights of Columbus Indoor Track Meet. After Mark Walsh and I finished our events, I suggested we stop by a nearby arcade. Mark hesitated, worried about not having any extra money. But I pulled out a stack of Dick Gregory bills from my back pocket and reassured him that I had his back. We spent the evening playing pinball machines and laughing as we exchanged those novelty bills for quarters. Dick Gregory did not do well in the presidential contest, but to this day, Mark (now Dr. Walsh) still fondly recalls the fun we had with those Gregory dollars.

In May 1969, as the school year drew to a close, I found myself reflecting on a successful academic and athletic semester. I earned All-American titles in both indoor and outdoor sprints, an honor that required finishing in the top six of NCAA national competitions. Sportswriters were optimistic about my chances of making the U.S. Olympic team, especially since I had previously set a world record in the 300-yard dash indoors.

As I prepared for the upcoming trials, I felt the pressure mount. Many believed I was a better fit for the 200 meters than the 100 meters. In the semifinal heat for the 100 meters, I finished third, which meant I advanced to the finals. All I needed to do was finish in the top four in the finals to secure a spot on the Olympic 4 x 100-meter relay team.

When the final race came, I finished fifth. The top four

runners were Jim Hines from Texas Southern, Charlie Green from Nebraska, Mel Pender from the U.S. Army, and Ronnie Ray Smith from San Jose State. They went on to win the gold medal in the 4x100 relay at the 1968 Olympic Games in Mexico City.

While I was disappointed that I would not qualify for the relay team, my spirits remained high at the thought of competing in my favorite event, the 200-meter sprint. I won my heats in both the quarter-finals and semifinals, but then fate dealt me a cruel blow. I pulled a muscle in the 200-meter semi-final and was unable to compete any further. I was one sprint away from the Olympics, just 200 yards between me and the greatest track event on earth, and I had to watch the dream slip away through my fingers.

That felt like a crushing defeat at the time, but looking back now, I realize how fortunate I was to even be considered among the best athletes this country had to offer. Though I never tried out for the Olympic team again, I cherish my time in those competitions as an unexpected adventure, one that I never envisioned for myself but am forever grateful for. After all, I had just barely missed earning a coveted spot on the 1968 U.S. Olympic Track & Field Team.

I will always take pride in having left my footprint at Notre Dame. I have two remaining sprinting records, though both of these are no longer part of Notre Dame's official all-time list simply because my events were run in yards instead of meters (there's an ongoing petition to convert these distances from yards to meters, which could place me at the top of the all-time list for indoor 60 meters). I cherish my journey as a student-athlete and hope that my experiences can inspire future generations. I like to think that my presence has contributed to the university's increased diversity. Notre Dame now admits many more Black men and women who excel academically while also succeeding in extracurricular activities.

If you visit the new Harris Track & Field Stadium at the corner of Leahy Drive and Edison Road, you'll see my name on the all-time Track & Field record board for both the 100 and 200 meters. However, a less visible mark is the growing number of talented and bright Black students and faculty who have been given the opportunity to demonstrate their worth. This progress has made Notre Dame a more diverse and desirable institution of higher learning, helping it maintain its mission and solidify its position among the nation's top universities.

PART III
1969–1980

CHAPTER 10
BOSTON

In May of 1969, I finished Notre Dame with many great memories in mind and an engineering college degree in my hand. I was unsure about my next career move, but I had options. The market value of an electrical engineering (E.E.) degree from Notre Dame was high. I also learned that several of my E.E. classmates were pursuing advanced graduate degrees in non-engineering disciplines, such as Masters of Business Administration (M.B.A.), law degrees (J.D.), or medical degrees (M.D.). Many subjects within electrical engineering rely heavily on logical and analytical thinking, making it a very versatile degree to pursue. This is one of the reasons why E.E. graduates have successful careers in other disciplines.

Upon graduation, I earned an NCAA postgraduate award for being an honor student-athlete. I contemplated using the award to attend Columbia University in New York City. It was a dream to attend Columbia after visiting New York a few years prior. However, I eventually decided to enter the workforce. I accepted a position with General Electric Jet Engines Facility as a systems engineer in Lynn, Massachusetts, a small coastal town just seven miles north of downtown Boston.

A significant factor in my job hunt was the ongoing Vietnam War. In 1969, the United States was deeply involved in the conflict, and U.S. Federal Law required nearly all male citizens and immigrants aged eighteen to twenty-five to register with Selective Service. With a low draft number, there was a high likelihood that I would be drafted into the military. As a Black man, I was particularly concerned because several of my friends had already lost their lives in the war. Plus, Black men were drafted in disproportionately high numbers, so there was a higher probability that I would be conscripted simply due to my race. However, I could avoid the draft by working for a company with a military contract, as this employment provided me with an exemption.

Another significant appeal of this job was its proximity to Rhynette. Lynn was only about a two-hour drive to Mt Holyoke College in South Hadley, where Rhynette was starting her junior year. Despite the political turmoil of the time and the tragedy of these global conflicts, this was a hopeful time for me, personally. I had a college degree, a good job, and a nice car. I was living in an exciting new city. I found an apartment with Harold Tate from Cincinnati, who was also an engineer and, coincidentally, later became a physician.

Perhaps most importantly, I was able to see Rhynette regularly, and we became more serious in our relationship. There was a lot to be happy about, and by the summer of 1970, I realized that I was irrevocably in love with Rhynette. I could not see my future without her by my side. She was smart, funny, beautiful, loyal, and generous. She had captured my heart. After a year with General Electric, I saved enough money to buy Rhynette a ring, and before long, we were not only inseparable—we were engaged to be married.

Becoming a husband and a father were now the biggest goals in my life. I aspired to be everything my parents were and even more. Their love and guidance shaped my vision of family, and I was eager to create a life that reflected that legacy. We planned a large church wedding back home in Memphis.

The wedding took place on a humid, warm, sunny Memphis day, June 6, 1970, at the Evergreen Presbyterian Church. The church was a striking white structure, exuding an austere beauty with its tall windows and grand gables. It was the perfect afternoon, as a slight breeze blew to cool our guests. Rhynette and I had four bridesmaids and groomsmen, with my brother Leon being my best man. As the doors opened to the church, I finally saw Rhynette for the first time in almost two days. Dressed in her long white wedding gown, she looked like an angel. I fought back tears at the sight of her and as the magnitude of the situation pressed upon me. I wanted to keep it together for my own sake and Rhynette's. I was sure if she saw me crying, she would lose it, too.

Much like during a sprint, time seemed to slow down and speed up at the same time. Images of the ceremony flashed past me, and sounds of music and singing lingered in my ears. Unlike in a race, I was already standing at the finish line with the greatest prize a person could win. Before I knew it, Rhynette and I were married.

After years of courtship, long-distance romance, and happy reunions, I was finally married to that lovely girl who had peered around the corner of the music room as I played my saxophone back at Manassas High. I was shell-shocked in the loveliest way.

A beautiful, quaint reception followed the ceremony. We danced and drank the night away as I held my lovely wife for the first of many times to come.

After the wedding, we relocated to Boston, where Rhynette could complete her senior year coursework remotely for Mount Holyoke, and I would start grad school at the MIT Sloan School of Management. Together, we were embarking on a new and exciting journey as a young married couple.

We quickly made new friends in our apartment building, which was home to five other Black graduate and medical students from the nearby Tufts Medical School. Most of these medical students hailed from Tougaloo College in Jackson, Mississippi. We were all around the same age and shared a similar background, growing up in a segregated Southern environment, which fostered an immediate connection among us. Rhynette completed her coursework at Simmons College and earned her undergraduate degree from Mount Holyoke College in 1971. She then enrolled in Harvard's one-year M.A.T. (Master of Arts in Teaching) program.

On May 6, 1972, our first son, Bill Jr., was born at St. Elizabeth's Hospital in Brighton, Massachusetts, near Boston. At that point, we were both graduate students, newlyweds, and new parents, all while managing on a limited income. As challenging as that may have seemed, it was undoubtedly one of the most exciting and happy times in our lives. I worked part-time while also teaching at MIT to help keep our cash flow steady. Rhynette had started graduate school at Harvard and juggled her family responsibilities while pursuing her degree.

To this day, I'm not sure how we managed to support a newborn and a growing family on such a small budget and tight schedule, but somehow, we made it work. Not only that, we were truly happy. We listened to music and played cards with friends. We had our favorite little seafood and Greek restaurants in Harvard Square. There was also the camaraderie of other young Black families who shared our experiences, which made the journey a bit easier. We all lived in the same apartment complex at 474 Tremont Street, just a stone's throw from downtown Boston and Tufts Medical School. Most of our apartment building neighbors were at Tufts Medical School down the street, while a few were navigating paths at MIT alongside me.

One MIT Sloan School classmate and grad student who became a lifelong friend is Fred Toney from Pine Bluff, Arkansas. He and I share the same interests in music, tennis, economics, and E-trading. Fred is a former Economics professor at Lemoyne-Owen College, now residing back home in Pine Bluff, making sometimes challenging efforts to stimulate declining economic development in his hometown. We visit each other often as he is still one of my closest and most trusted friends.

Another lifelong friend is Dr. James H. Williams, Jr., now a professor of Mechanical Engineering and professor of Writing and Humanistic Studies. He is a prolific writer and researcher and has received several teaching awards at MIT. He and I developed a lasting friendship as we shared similar interests, hobbies, and backgrounds. To this day, I look forward to visiting him in Boston to play golf and hang out.

Many of the couples, like Rhynette and me, were also raising young children, and none of us had outside jobs to fall back on. We were in the constant pursuit of education and happiness. Boston became our haven for following our dreams with like-minded individuals, simultaneously giving us community, hope, and fun.

The music scene in Boston was ideal for the free self-expression of our great American art form, jazz. The Berklee School of Music near downtown Boston provided a constant source of musical inspiration for gigs and practice sessions with Berkelee's students and faculty. The draw of the Berklee scene was a gravitational pull that I could not resist. I hung out around Berkelee so much that people began to think I was a student there. This music scene featured some of the most skilled and creative players I had ever been around. It challenged me to develop my own skills and style further, moving past anything I had been taught before. When I reflect on my time in Boston, it seems like a musical renaissance that turned me into the serious musical artist I am today.

I played alto sax in the MIT Jazz Band, directed by Herb Pomeroy, the late Berkelee professor and trumpeter. Together, we traveled to Switzerland for the 1970 Montreux Jazz Festival, along with guest artist Clark Terry, who performed on the trumpet with us. Rhynette, who was usually very supportive of my different goals and pursuits, wasn't especially happy about this trip since it occurred right after our wedding, and we could not afford the travel expenses for her to come along. The band played beautifully, though, for a crowd of European jazz lovers. After our festival performance, two of my bandmates rented a car to go on a short sight-seeing tour. They invited me to tag along, and we drove from Montreux, which is near the Swiss-French border, up into the mountains. We took small twisting roads through the gorgeous scenery and small villages. It was an idyllic adventure—until we tried to retrace our steps to get back to Montreux. We had become hopelessly lost on these small Alpine highways and roads. We finally ended up in a small town in Northern France, where we found a restaurant and met a group of locals who directed us back to the Swiss border and Montreux. We were young and adventurous, and it was fun.

A year later, it was also a thrill to travel with the MIT Jazz Ensemble to the Notre Dame Collegiate Jazz Festival in 1971. It was not quite as exciting as getting lost in the Alpines, but I loved returning to campus, reconnecting with instructors and friends, and showing off the campus to my MIT bandmates.

During my time in Boston, I had the great fortune of meeting Charles Curl, a Harvard law student and undergraduate who has remained a close friend and collaborator to this day. When we're together, we inspire each other in ways that feel electric, whether it's playing music or having a conversation. You can almost hear our neurons firing as we dive into a song or a topic. One of us will bring up an idea, and the other will chime in, sharing our thoughts, and we never cease to learn from each other. It's a dialogue that feels rare and special, a real exchange of knowledge and creativity.

We formed a jazz group in Cambridge and performed regularly within the MIT-Harvard community. Our musical collaboration has continued to this day. Charles now lives in Hilton Head, South Carolina, with his wife Yvonne, a retired Xerox executive. Their home, which Charles helped design, features a state-of-the-art music recording home studio. Together, Charles and I have produced four albums, and one of them, *Return of the Hip*, reached number one on the Jazz Lovers WUMR 91.7 FM Top 10 Countdown, a nationally syndicated jazz radio station based at the University of Memphis, and remained there for several weeks. By the way, this recording (*Return of the Hip*) can be accessed on Spotify under the name "Curl and Hurd".

We continue to work on musical projects that require frequent trips to Hilton Head, where we also make time for golf and tennis. Like me, Charles is deeply focused and committed to all his endeavors. He also maintains a friendship with the owner of the popular Hilton Head venue, The Jazz Corner. The house band, including pianist and bandleader Lavon Stevens, has always been generous in inviting me to sit-in on saxophone during my visits, and twice, I have had the pleasure of performing as a guest artist.

At one of these performances in the spring of 2019, Charles and Leon had a surprise in store for me. In the middle of my performance, just before the beginning of the next song, a man with his baritone saxophone walked onto the small band stage. Lavon introduced him as Leon Rivchun and then announced to the audience that Leon and I were both MIT graduates and played in the MIT Jazz Ensemble together.

Me, Leon Rivchun, and Charles Curl

My memory of Leon was vague. I was then a graduate student, while Leon was an undergraduate architecture student. Nevertheless, that night at the Jazz Corner began a wonderful reconnection and friendship. It was a beautiful illustration of how paths cross and how music brings people together. On my frequent trips to Hilton Head, Charles and I always arrange to get with Leon and enjoy jam sessions that last for hours. Leon has a very impressive collection of twenty-five vintage saxophones, most of which he has repaired. I have purchased two of these instruments from him. Most sax players would appreciate the joy that Charles, Leon, and I experience spending hours experimenting with different reeds, mouthpieces, ligatures, and saxophones in our attempts to create different sounds. This is a never-ending work in progress. Music introduced me to friends like Charles and Leon, but it was inevitable to learn that we had so much else in common, too.

At Notre Dame, I had set out to take advantage of all it had to offer and leave with no regrets. Similarly, I wanted to immerse myself in all Boston offered. The jazz music scene was thriving, with MIT frequently hosting artists and musicians. In 1970, jazz tenor saxophonist Joe Henderson, one of my favorites, performed at MIT. I secured a front-row seat and eagerly anticipated speaking with him after the performance.

While chatting with Mr. Henderson, I was interrupted by a loud voice from the audience: "Hey, Bill Hurd from Memphis!" Although momentarily frustrated to cut my conversation short, I was intrigued to discover that someone in the audience might be from Memphis and possibly know me. It turned out to be Michael (Mike) Fant. We immediately hit it off, both of us glad to find fellow Memphians here in Boston. He and I would be friends in several different cities together over the years, including Memphis, Boston, and Nashville. Mike had attended Mitchell Road High in Memphis before becoming an MIT undergraduate. I completed my graduate studies at MIT in 1972, and Mike finished his undergraduate degree in 1973. Before he graduated, he became friends with another Black MIT undergraduate named Ron McNair, who went on to become the second Black astronaut in history when he went to space in 1984. Tragically, Ron died in the 1986 Space Shuttle Challenger disaster, but he left behind an amazing and lasting legacy.

Attending MIT was truly a unique experience in an international city with an abundance of prestigious colleges and universities. It seemed like every undergrad student I met was either a high school valedictorian or had scored a perfect 800 on the SAT—or both. This created an intellectual atmosphere that was both stimulating and challenging, and I was constantly inspired to explore ideas and my own creativity in many different ways. World-renowned professors resided in almost every campus building. For example, Dr. Amar Bose was a professor of electrical engineering and computer science at MIT from 1959 to 2001. He was the founder of the Bose Corporation, which supplies audio speakers worldwide and to many automotive companies. Dr. Jay Forrester was a professor of digital computing and systems dynamics, and his office was located adjacent to a classroom I attended regularly at the Sloan School of Management. Dr. Forrester invented the random-access magnetic core memory, the information storage device employed in most digital computers. This technology was important in the development of Artificial Intelligence.

I participated in regular brainstorming sessions with a group of seven Black graduate students from MIT and Harvard. There were three Harvard medical students, two MIT Sloan students, and two students from the Harvard Business School. These "skull sessions" were thought-provoking, creative, and sometimes esoteric—but always fascinating. I looked forward to these gatherings with great anticipation. More than just conversations, we also took on some meaningful challenges. Together, we were able to secure two small National Science Foundation grants to study nutritional deficits of specific diets in Roxbury and neighboring Black communities. There seemed to be an atmosphere in Boston for this kind of brainstorming and activity that is rarely found in a city like Memphis.

During the final year of my graduate studies, I focused my master's thesis on creating a computer simulation model of a Boston food cooperative system. The proposed objective was to determine what parameters influence the operating efficiency and the individual family food cost savings of a community food co-op. The computer simulation model that I constructed (written in the COBOL computer programming language) predicted the outcome of the Co-op's operation with a high degree of accuracy and certainty, to the point that the Co-op Group installed my model for fulltime use to maximize its efficiency and optimize its overall operation. I felt honored.

My time in Boston was a cornucopia of experiences: pursuing my graduate degree, enjoying family life, collaborating with musicians, and continuing to compete in track events. My days of competing in collegiate track meets were behind me, but not my desire to continue running. From 1969–1972, I continued to compete as a track & field athlete.

Winning a 100 meter race in a Boston area track meet

I ran in local track meets, trained with the infamous sprinter/hematologist Dr. Delano Meriweather, and ran for the Philadelphia Pioneer Track club, coached by the very personable and capable Alex Woodley. On several occasions, he would call to see if my passport was up to date, then proceed to send me from Boston to Italy, Stuttgart, London, or Trinidad for International or AAU Track Meets. It was a true joy to keep competing at these high levels, travel the world, and soar across those finish lines.

In all, Boston in the early 1970s was a time and place of excitement and fulfillment for me. But, as they say, all things come to an end.

CHAPTER 11
NASHVILLE

After graduating from the MIT Sloan School of Management master's program, I found myself facing the same question as I did when I left Notre Dame. Where do I go from here? Once again, I had strong credentials and plenty of opportunities. However, this time, I was a married man with a small child. Rhynette and I enjoyed our time in Boston immensely, everything from the long study sessions to connecting with friends and colleagues and enjoying life-changing experiences. We loved the international flavor and the metropolitan side of Boston. But Boston had two downsides: the unforgiving cold and snowy winters and the long distances between us and our families, which became even more pronounced now that we had a family of our own. So, ultimately, we decided to leave Boston and find a city with warmer weather and closer to family.

Instead of enrolling in a joint MIT-Harvard Bioengineering PhD program, I accepted a consulting job heading a Minority Business Training Center in Nashville with the stipulation that I would also teach management courses in the Business Administration Department at Tennessee State University (TSU). Rhynette received a teaching position at Middle Tennessee State University (MTSU). Everything seemed to fall into place despite our mixed emotions about leaving Boston.

Rhynette and I found a great deal on a foreclosed house and were able to purchase it for well under market value. The California-style build was unique to this area, with a winding circular driveway, a waterfall just inside the front door entrance, and a large skylight above the waterfall. It was a convenient location for our commutes to work, too. We would soon find out that we lived not far from Fred Thompson, the former U.S. senator from Tennessee and actor on the *Law and Order* TV series. They lived in a more upscale part of the Brentwood neighborhood, home to various Country and Western celebrities I had heard of but never met. More importantly, his wife was a professor at MTSU with Rhynette, and they would carpool together.

While I enjoyed the neighborhood and scenery that accompanied it, I frequently found myself stopped by Brentwood police for reasons I termed "Driving While Black." This racial profiling became so frustrating that I filed a written complaint at the nearby police precinct. Unfortunately, nothing came of it, and the unjustified traffic stops continued. After asking for my license and registration, the officers would often follow up with questions like, "What business do you have here?" or "Why are you in Brentwood?" or even, "Is this your Mercedes?"

When I shared my experiences of constant racial profiling

with my White friends, many of them didn't believe me or made excuses for why it might be happening. A few were sympathetic, but most of them were completely insulated from this form of racism and couldn't even imagine it, especially in the 70s and 80s. It wasn't until the 1990s, after Rodney King was beaten by Los Angeles police officers and the city was consumed by riots, that people began to pay more attention to these kinds of racial profiling and police brutality events. But even now, it persists. Even if you're Barack Obama or LeBron James, a racist person only sees the color of your skin.

I don't believe children are born with hate or racial bias. Rather, it stems from environmental influences and upbringing. Many of my White classmates at Notre Dame often shared their backgrounds with me. Typically, their parents voted Republican, considered themselves conservative, attended private or Catholic schools, and had few, if any, Black friends. My family was like a mirror image: we voted along Democratic lines, went to public schools, attended protestant churches, and had very few White friends and neighbors.

Upon arriving in Nashville, I got involved in the incubation of minority business ventures. Many of my clients were in the healthcare field, including several Black physicians. One of these collaborations led to the establishment of a minority-owned and operated medical center. I utilized my management skills to help develop the investment package for a Medical Center for Women's Health. Although all six investors were based in Nashville, the Medical Center was in Memphis. We hired two board-certified obstetricians/gynecologists and a staff. Each investor contributed $4,000 in starting capital, and I had to take a loan from the bank to contribute my share.

To our surprise and delight, the clinic was an immediate financial success. So much so it only took me a few weeks to return the money I borrowed from the bank. During the infancy stages of the project, I was sure it would garner success, but even I was taken aback by the immediate achievement. What's more, having worked so closely with these healthcare professionals and seeing firsthand the need for the care they were providing, I became very interested in the healthcare field myself. This experience planted the seed that would blossom into an amazing forty-year career, but it would still take me some time to realize it.

Another great joy of living in Nashville was reconnecting with Mike Fant, my friend from MIT. He had become the first Black student to enter Vanderbilt's six-year M.D.-Ph.D. program. It was refreshing to have a fellow Memphian and friend who shared my interests and scientific mindset. He also played alto saxophone, like I did. We still laugh about how he often tried but failed to "cut my head," a Memphis term meaning to outplay someone musically.

We had all kinds of fun together. One time, Mike was interested in a charming Black bank teller. One day, while hanging out, we drove up to her drive-through window in Mike's light blue VW hatchback—definitely not a "playa's whip." Even worse, we were dressed casually in T-shirts. Mike took this moment to ask for her phone number and was immediately turned down with an "I don't know you!" response.

We returned to Mike's apartment and, combining our

scientific and analytical minds, devised a plan to impress the bank teller. I suggested he don his medical school white coat and take my parked Jaguar back to the bank, driving alone. I stayed at his apartment. A short while later, Mike returned with a big grin and showed me her name and phone number written on a piece of notepad paper from the bank.

Pioneering Biologist on Joining MIT Universe
A retired physician-scientist known for pioneering research in placental biology, Michael Fant '73 reflects on his time exploring the Institute.

Mike Fant, M.D.

Now retired and living in Tampa Bay with his lovely wife Ana Maria, Mike held tenured professorships at the University of Texas at Houston and the University of South Florida in Tampa. I am currently helping him get back into playing alto saxophone, though he feels it may put him in an unlikely position to "cut my head." I told him, "Good luck with that, Mike."

My music career continued seamlessly in Nashville, where I formed a band with the talented musicians Louis Taylor on piano (from St. Thomas, U.S. Virgin Islands), Ben Jones on trumpet (from El Dorado, Arkansas), Johnny "Cool" Johnson on drums (from northern Mississippi), Ed Moon on bass (from Nashville, Tennessee), and Walter "Heart Attack" King, B.B. King's nephew, on tenor sax (from Memphis, Tennessee). We performed extensively across Nashville, a city then predominantly known for Country & Western music. Pianist Louis Taylor and I opened for notable artists, including singer Melba Moore, pianist Joe Sample (formerly of the Jazz Crusaders), and alto saxophonist David Sanborn. Nashville became my third music sanctuary, a place to explore my sound and tap into the unique swinging musical scene that only the South truly had. I was definitely back home, musically, but in a strange and utterly different way.

Having taken my music to the next level professionally, I had the pleasure of performing and collaborating with even more amazing artists like bassist Ed Dungey and trumpeters Ben Jones and William Fielder. In 1974, my band was invited to perform at the Notre Dame Collegiate Jazz Festival, and once more, I had the thrill of returning to my alma mater to reconnect and play music. From 1972 to 1980, we played at several collegiate events for Tennessee State University, Fisk University, and Meharry Medical College.

Of course, there were challenging times, too, and one of the most difficult moments was when my father passed away at the VA Hospital in Memphis. He was just fifty-four years old and died due to complications from diabetes. This was devastating news. My father had been the heart and soul of the family for decades. He had supported me through thick and thin. And now he was gone, far too soon.

Years later, as an ophthalmology chief resident at that very hospital, I sought out and reviewed his medical records in the VA archives. There, I uncovered the heartbreaking truth: his death was caused by a new medication being tested, oral hypoglycemics, which caused severe liver toxicity followed by liver failure.

CHAPTER 12
MEDICAL SCHOOL

My life in Nashville became a time of reflection and consideration. I had earned many different credentials up to now, but I was plagued by the question, "Who do I want to be?" I was happy with my family, my music, and my work with minority businesses and teaching. Still, I felt that something was missing. I wasn't achieving my full potential.

For years, I had been searching for a discipline that would engage my mechanical mind, so I was sure that working in technology was the best option for me. After researching programs at Vanderbilt University, I enrolled in their Ph.D. program in Artificial Intelligence (A.I.). However, I was unable to finish my program due to a lack of interest. During my time at MIT Sloan School, I was exposed to a more sophisticated version of A.I. through the work of Dr. Jay W. Forrester. So, the Vanderbilt experience never fully captured my attention.

In the meantime, I kept thinking of my work with the Medical

Center for Women's Health and the other physicians I had worked with, helping to launch their projects. By now, I had relationships with multiple Meharry-trained physicians and witnessed their ability to heal sick patients. I admired their calm, respectable demeanors. I realized that a career in medicine was becoming more and more intriguing to me.

There was another incident that influenced me to become a physician. A friend who I played tennis with regularly at Nashville's Hadley Park Tennis Center, was trying to get into medical school, but was unsuccessful on two attempts to pass the Medical College Admissions Test (MCAT). He asked for my help. So, we gathered copies of several past MCAT tests, and spent several weeks in rigorous study. We also spent a lot of time examining standardized test-taking techniques to the point where he passed his next MCAT with flying colors, gaining immediate admission to medical school. This experience of helping a friend get into medical school gave me reason to believe that I could get into medical school as well.

So, during my medical school application process, I was invited for a pre-admission interview, which is typically a positive step toward acceptance. Near the end of the interview, the elderly gentleman, who I later learned was a retired Black physician, remarked, "I see here on your resume that you are also a jazz musician, young man. You can't be a serious physician if you are a jazz musician." He then asked, "Are you prepared to give up music to pursue medicine?"

My immediate, unspoken reaction was, *Are you kidding me?! And by the way, jazz is a serious American art form.*

He seemed to believe that physicians should devote their entire lives solely to medicine and have no outside interests or hobbies. I strongly disagreed and conveyed to him that music was an integral part of my life, and I would not give it up.

It turns out I was not accepted to that school, but placed on a waiting list for admission. Years later, medical school admissions officers would change their tune and favor applicants with diverse backgrounds, including interests in the fine arts, but in the 1970s, this was considered a negative quality.

Having settled in Nashville, Meharry Medical School became the next logical choice. Not only was I impressed with the physicians I had met from their program, but it was an HBCU (Historically Black Colleges and Universities), which was both refreshing and comfortable. I felt truly at home among Black intellectual peers, and I was excited about the prospects of being able to improve the health and well-being of others. With a lot of work and my strong credentials from Notre Dame and MIT, I was accepted.

I entered Meharry Medical College in the fall of 1976 at age twenty-nine. The average medical school freshman was twenty-two. I think this was one of the reasons I was elected Freshman class president, a role I was honored to have in my first year in medical school. This title encouraged me to persevere when things got tough and gave me a push whenever studying became a challenge as I balanced all the commitments in my life. I was now a medical student, a proud father to Bill Jr., and a happily married husband to my intelligent and beautiful wife, Rhynette. Life was certainly hectic as she and I were pulled in separate directions very often. One thing we always loved to do together, though, was support Bill Jr. When he was old enough, he started playing Pop Warner football, and we had a great time cheering him on from the sidelines. He played half-back and wore number thirty-three, hoping to channel some of Tony Dorsett's magic. To this day, Bill Jr. is still a diehard Dallas Cowboy fan.

Thanks to my previous investments and business ventures, such as the Medical Center for Women's Health, I was fortunate to focus on medical school without financial concerns. I had saved enough to cover my medical education, avoiding the burden of student loans that many of my classmates faced from undergraduate studies and medical school. I had no student loans from Notre Dame or MIT, as I received full athletic and academic scholarships. Additionally, I now earned a small but steady income as an adjunct professor at Fisk University and from frequent musical gigs. Reflecting on my medical school experience, I believe the lack of financial worries and stress contributed greatly to my success in school and my personal life.

Medical school demanded most of my time because of the vast amount of information to digest and master. Despite the intensity, it was a thrilling and rewarding phase of my life. Each day offered new insights, and I enjoyed finding similarities between the human body and the principles of engineering. My brain felt like it was saturated with information, but for the first time, I felt I was pursuing the perfect career path. This was the piece that had been missing before, and I was truly excited about the prospect of being able to improve people's lives.

I remember the first course of my first year, Gross Anatomy, as if it were yesterday: walking into the stark white basement classroom, recoiling from the smell, and shivering in the winter-like air that blasted from the air conditioners. Five first-year medical students were assigned to each cadaver, which was to be completely dissected and studied over the first semester. My team included Bryan Washington, Dennis Carter, Sheila Allison, Fred Burton, and me. The smell of formaldehyde filled the room, leaving some of us nauseated and teary-eyed. This organic compound was widely used as a tissue preservative and embalming fluid. Of course, formaldehyde was later banned in classroom settings like this because of its carcinogenic properties, but we were immersed in it multiple times per week. To this day, if I smell even a whiff of formaldehyde, I'm immediately transported back to that basement classroom full of cadavers.

After the first week or so in the Gross Anatomy Room, it became more tolerable. Our anatomy professor, Dr. John Norris, was an amazing and kind teacher who encouraged our curiosity. He later became a friend outside the classroom, and we discovered we had a shared admiration for fine automobiles. He had a particular passion for vintage British cars and one afternoon, he invited me to his home to view his collection. I was utterly amazed at the condition, as well as the variety of his cars. I had never seen such an impressive collection of restored British and vintage automobiles. One car in his collection that especially captured my attention was a 1960 Jaguar XK S 3.8 Liter Coupe, a white two-door with wire rims. It was in mint condition, almost like something you'd see at a car show.

During this first year, I heard about a Student Research Day competition, but I was so overwhelmed with demanding courses like Gross Anatomy and Physiology that I couldn't find the time to prepare something. I decided to wait until my second year to participate. Drawing from my experience at MIT, where I developed software for the computer model of a Boston Food Coop for my master's thesis, I came up with the idea for a new project: a computer simulation of a clinical diagnosis model.

This system allowed users to input symptoms, such as right lower quadrant pain, fever, nausea, vomiting, or elevated white blood count. The computer model then generated potential diagnoses like acute appendicitis or cholecystitis. The more symptoms and lab results entered, the more precise the diagnosis became. Similar to artificial intelligence, the model improved with use, expanding its database and "learning" over time, much like a computer chess program that evaluates every possible move.

Not only did my classmates find my clinical diagnosis model impressive, but some faculty members at Meharry were equally enthusiastic. I was honored to win first place in the 1977 Meharry Student Research Day competition.

During my third year of medical school, we began seeing clinical patients on the hospital wards and started considering which specialty to pursue. The late Dr. Axel Hansen, who served as the Chairman of the Department of Ophthalmology at Meharry Medical College from 1960 until his death in 2008, was instrumental in my decision to choose ophthalmology.

Dr. Hansen must have noticed my enthusiasm during my

ophthalmology rotation. Early in the rotation, he introduced me to the basics of the specialty. With a patient in his office, Dr. Hansen placed a lighted indirect ophthalmoscope around my head and guided my hand to position a biconvex lens. I was amazed to see a panoramic view of the retina and optic nerve in the back of the patient's eye. My background in optics, physics, and engineering only served to pique my interest even more. I was officially sold on ophthalmology.

Dr. Hansen was not only a consummate professional with a soft-spoken Caribbean accent and warm bedside manner but also a prolific scholar. He authored over thirty scientific articles, made numerous presentations, and wrote two books while heading the Department of Ophthalmology at Meharry. His expertise and willingness to share his time and knowledge left a lasting impression on me.

Meharry Medical College allowed third-year medical students to attend two externships away from campus, offering a valuable opportunity to explore and assess potential specialties. For my first externship, I returned to Boston to extern at the Massachusetts Eye and Ear Hospital, an ophthalmology residency program affiliated with Harvard University. Despite the biting cold weather, I was excited to return to Boston to explore ophthalmology with some of the best ophthalmologists in the nation. For three weeks in the spring of 1978, I stayed with an old friend, John Thomas, a former Olympic silver medalist high jumper from Boston University. One evening, however, I got lost and found myself in South Boston, an area predominantly Irish Catholic and less diverse at the time. It was very dark except for a few streetlights. As I waited at a stoplight, three young white men approached my car. Before I could ask for directions, one of them yelled, "Nigga what are you doing here?" He pulled out a sharp object and struck my windshield, causing severe cracks.

Flooded with shock and anger, my first instinct was to fight. I wanted to jump out and confront my attackers. But my second and more powerful instinct was to survive. I understood I was outnumbered and would likely be harmed or worse if I left my car. So, despite my impulse to retaliate, I wisely drove away quickly. Live to fight another day, I told myself, but it was a cold comfort.

I was so accustomed to seeing and being the target of hatred and racial prejudice that one more episode did not surprise me. But that didn't make it any easier to swallow. I remembered how my dad responded to similar situations by keeping cool and allowing karma to rule. But I wanted to know how he dealt with the anger that accumulates over so many years. How did he deal with the feelings of helplessness when he couldn't retaliate against these people out of fear for his own life or those of his family?

My belief is that racist individuals are typically ignorant, have poor self-esteem, and lack self-confidence. Many have racist parents, and many are hateful and don't like the idea of disadvantaged people being given an opportunity to improve their lives. I do not like hearing the phrase, "We live by our own set of family values." What does that mean? Does it mean people who don't look like you don't have family values?

For my second externship, I chose the Bascom-Palmer Eye

Institute, a branch of the University of Miami. I selected it because of the elite status of its ophthalmology residency program. In Miami, my host family was Gloria and Hubbard Alexander, who had lived across the street from us in Nashville when I was just starting at Meharry. "Axe," as everyone called him, had been an assistant football coach at Vanderbilt. Axe, Gloria, and their two boys left Nashville for Miami, where Axe was now the wide receivers coach for the Miami Dolphins. Later, he would go to coach with the Dallas Cowboys and the Minnesota Vikings, and before retiring, he would be the head coach at Melrose High School in Memphis.

The two externships in Boston and Miami were important steps in solidifying my choice of ophthalmology as a specialty coming out of medical school. Both were nationally rated programs and were included in my wish list of potential landing spots for my residency.

However, a national matching system would ultimately determine where I would go.

PART IV
RETURNING HOME AS BILL HURD, M.D.

CHAPTER 13
INTERNSHIP AND RESIDENCY

Ophthalmology is a highly competitive specialty, with many medical students applying to multiple programs to secure a spot. I applied to only three programs nationally: Ochsner Clinic in New Orleans, Massachusetts Eye and Ear, and the University of Tennessee Health Science Center (UTHSC) in Memphis. I was matched with Ochsner Clinic and UTHSC. Rhynette and I explored Ochsner Clinic as she considered a teaching position at Tulane University, but after much deliberation, we ultimately decided to return home to Memphis, where I was honored to become one of the first Black residents in this UTHSC program alongside Dr. Brenda Jones from North Carolina.

Not only was this a terrific career opportunity, but it was also good for our family. Rhynette and I wanted our kids to have the same stability that our childhoods had offered. Moving back home was always something we thought about, and here was our chance. In our calculations, the pros of settling down amongst friends and family far outweighed the cons. So, on a warm sunny day in July 1980, we packed the family car for one last move and made the short trip from Nashville to Memphis. Upon driving into Memphis, I realized how much I missed the familiar smells and sounds of my childhood. It was a perfect reversal from my younger years when I spent so much time dreaming of cities and adventures far away from here. Now, I was thrilled to return to where all those dreams were born. I thought of that saying: All roads lead home. This was certainly true for me.

There were five matched residency positions at UTHSC out of over 600 national applicants. I believe UTHSC recognized my local connection to Memphis and the strength of my interview. In my graduating class of one hundred twenty-five students, only three of us, including Dr. Ronald McFarland in Nashville and Dr. Derek Dawson in Gary, Indiana, chose to pursue ophthalmology (and all three of us have had successful careers in the field).

Upon graduation, I felt sure I could handle any problems I might encounter during my residency. After all, I had survived Notre Dame, MIT, and medical school. What could possibly be more difficult than all of that? Well, let me tell you about another old saying that comes to mind: "When you make a plan, god laughs."

I was exceedingly wrong about being prepared for anything that UTHSC might throw at me. My experience there turned out to be the most difficult to adjust to, but not for academic or medical reasons. It was racism. I had never had to deal with so much of it, so consistently. In my all-Black high school, I was just another student in the classroom. At Notre Dame, I was a star athlete and top student. At MIT, people focused more on the intelligence of my ideas than the color of my skin. At Meharry, I was once more surrounded by Black peers and Instructors. But here I was now in a predominantly white medical program in the South, and I was beginning to realize just how big a challenge this was going to be.

It began during a general surgery rotation. I was the only Black physician in a scheduled Morbidity and Mortality (M&M) conference, and the head of the surgery department was conducting the class. He stood up and presented the medical-surgical case of a middle-aged Black female patient who was seated right there in the front of the classroom. The department head began by saying, "This is the case of a fifty-four-year-old Nigra Female presenting with…"

Before he could finish that sentence, my hand shot into the air, and I asked that he please use less derogatory descriptors, such as "Black" or "African American." This particular encounter ended agreeably enough as he took my suggestion and apologized. After the class, several doctors approached me and said I had "balls" to challenge the department head like that. That didn't seem like "balls" to me, though; it was common decency. Little did I know, but that was just the beginning of many incidents.

During my second year, I was serving as chief resident at the VA Hospital when I had a run-in with a first-year resident from South Carolina who was supposed to be under my direction. One of my responsibilities was to assign surgery cases to the first and second-year residents, but this particular first-year resident adamantly refused to take instructions from a Black man. When I reported the incident to the department chairman, Dr. Roger Hiatt, he smiled and assured me that there was no racism in his residency program. None. Furthermore, he informed me that I should be thankful I had been given the opportunity at UT in the first place.

Soon after this, I learned about some regular study sessions that my fellow residents were holding. We were all preparing for the Ophthalmology Board certification exams, but I learned that I was not invited to join these study sessions. I would be studying on my own.

And the hits kept coming. I had expressed an interest in doing a post-residency fellowship in corneal and refractive surgery, but those ambitions were soon dashed. I attended a lecture offered by a nationally renowned ophthalmologist who was the head of a prominent ophthalmology program, eager to learn more about his specialty. At the conclusion of his lecture, I went up and expressed my interest in becoming a fellow in his program. Without hesitation, he told me not even to bother applying. This elderly White physician had no idea who I was, what my credentials were, or even if I had already applied to his fellowship program. He took one look at me and made his harsh judgment based on whatever he saw and disapproved of.

Disheartened all around, I began to separate myself from the other residents, as well as from many of the faculty and staff. I showed up, did my job, and at the end of the day, I went home and got away from the hospital environment. I even began to question my choice of ophthalmology as a specialty. There seemed to be so much racism in this area, far more than my peers were facing in primary care specialties like pediatrics, family medicine, internal medicine or obstetrics and gynecology. After some deliberations, however, I determined not to allow this racism to change the course of my career. I knew I just had to finish this program, and I would be able to start a private practice in Memphis.

Another deeply motivating factor was seeing the reactions of Black nurses and patients as I made my rounds at John Gaston and the VA Hospitals. It was clear how excited and sometimes relieved they were to have a Black physician work with or treat them. I often heard how pleased they were to see someone who looked like them wearing the doctor's coat. Many of my Black patients commented on the level of respect and sincerity I offered them. These kinds of interactions inspired me to keep coming back, no matter how challenging the days were.

It has been my experience that treating patients' symptoms or performing surgery is the easy part. Treating *patients* is the hard part. Treating individuals like dignified human beings requires careful thought and kindness. There are no grades for thoughtfulness. Kindness is not taught in medical school. But I was raised in a family and community that held these qualities dear, and I was lucky to have inherited them.

Of course, that doesn't mean it's always easy to treat patients with dignity and respect, and I had some very tense encounters. To make extra money and develop my skills, I frequently moonlighted in Emergency Rooms in rural Arkansas, Mississippi, and Tennessee. This was in the 1980s, a time when the demand for ER doctors was high, and board certification in Emergency Medicine was not yet established. I obtained medical licenses in each of those states and was able to work in ERs on demand. Normally, I enjoyed the experience of treating patients and applying my medical knowledge, but some shifts were particularly challenging.

One night, while working alone in the ER at McNairy County Hospital in Selmer, Tennessee (the same hospital featured in the film *Walking Tall*), a middle-aged white man came into the ER with severe chest pains, collapsed in the ER lobby and went into full cardiac arrest. Three nurses and I worked tirelessly to restore his heartbeat, and after thirty minutes, we had him alive and stable. When it became clear that there were no family members present to identify him before his transfer to Intensive Care, I asked the nurse to check his pockets for identification. The first thing she pulled out was a Ku Klux Klan membership card. As the patient, still heavily sedated, regained consciousness and saw me, his immediate reaction was, "Who is this nigger and what is he doing here?" I tried to maintain my composure to avoid escalating the situation, but apparently, the anger showed on my face. The nurses quickly intervened, calming both the patient and me. They tried to explain to this man that I had just led the team that saved his life, but all I saw in his eyes was hate.

I would be lying if I said I never had doubts. All these experiences definitely made me question my decisions and whether or not I was strong enough to persevere through all of the racial behavior. At the end of the day, however, I stuck with my core convictions. As hard as it can be sometimes, I try not to consider another person's personal beliefs when they need help. In that moment, I am not concerned about a patient who is against same-sex marriage, or who is against abortion rights, or who has issues with other people's religion or beliefs. I feel strongly that most of these issues should be categorized as private and personal. As a physician, you hope that your patients will check their non-medical problems and political and religious beliefs at the door, and you do your best if they don't. The first objective is to treat and heal people.

Likewise, as a patient, you would hope for the same from your healthcare professionals. Many years later, I did not like it when I found myself a cancer patient sitting in the office of an oncologist who opened our session by asking me, "Do you know the Lord Jesus Christ?"

At first, his question was so unexpected I was speechless. With as much respect as I could muster, I eventually replied, "That's personal."

There were a lot of trials and challenges to overcome during my UTHSC residency, but there were also some terrific accomplishments and experiences. While there, I developed and constructed a prototype device for the microscopic measurement of certain inner parts of the human eye. I was granted both U.S. and foreign patents for this slit-lamp mountable intraocular biometer. I consulted an attorney friend, Sandy Chamblee, in Washington, D.C., who referred me to a specialized law firm focusing on medical device patents. After many months and significant legal fees, the patent attorneys laid the legal groundwork that led to the patents. During their international search for similar devices, they discovered a small West German company with a similar device design, but mine was unique in being mountable onto a slit lamp. The slit lamp is a microscope that uses a narrow beam of light to examine specific parts of the eye while the patient's chin is positioned to stabilize the head. To this day, I frequently receive inquiries from individuals seeking advice on how to patent their own ideas and inventions.

I also experienced my first medical mission trip when Dr. Jerre Freeman, the founder of the Memphis Eye and Cataract Association (MECA), led a team, including a few UTHSC ophthalmology residents, on a ten-day surgical mission trip to Ometepec, Mexico, usually around Thanksgiving. Ometepec is a small, rural city located about one hundred miles north of Acapulco, and the residents of this area had limited access to medical care, particularly ophthalmic healthcare. This was a transformative experience, and I would dedicate myself to many more mission trips in the future.

During the latter part of my residency, I focused a lot of attention on developing surgical skills by observing staff surgery cases. That's when I became close to Dr. Ralph Hamilton Sr. He turned out to be one of the few staff doctors who showed me kindness and generously shared his surgical techniques with me. I learned a great deal from him. While it is well-known that he donated millions of dollars to establish the Hamilton Eye Institute in Memphis, it may not be as widely known that he also made significant donations to Rust College in Holly Springs, Mississippi, a Historically Black College and University (HBCU).

During my thirty-six years of practice, I performed hundreds of strabismus procedures, corneal transplants, and oculoplastic surgeries. These procedures are typically carried out by ophthalmologists who have completed a one or two-year fellowship. However, thanks to Dr. Hamilton's generous guidance, I became proficient in these specialized procedures. Our friendship grew even closer after my residency. Towards the end of his life in 2017, I visited him for what turned out to be the last time. I didn't realize I was saying goodbye to a lifetime of friendship and mentorship in those last moments we shared. I remain deeply grateful for a relationship that few could experience.

CHAPTER 14
MEDICAL PRACTICE

Finally, I was in business. My ophthalmology practice grew rapidly from the very start due to a variety of factors. My celebrated and well-publicized athletic achievements bolstered my reputation in Memphis, but most importantly, many local physicians began referring patients. I operated from a main office at Methodist Hospital and had two satellite offices in Somerville, Tennessee, and in Holly Springs, Mississippi, at Dr. Kenneth Williams' minority-owned hospital. I performed eye surgeries at all three locations.

Treating cataract patients is the bulk of what general ophthalmologists do. Cataracts develop primarily from aging, generally starting when people are around fifty. A crystalline lens the size of a small button is located in the center of the eye, just behind the pupil, and functions like a prism directing light and images to the retina. When this clear lens becomes cloudy and opacified due to aging, eye injuries, overexposure to ultraviolet sunlight, or long-term systemic steroid use, eyesight becomes compromised.

A mature cataract usually requires a microsurgical procedure to remove and replace the clouded lens with an intraocular lens (IOL) implant. Modern-day cataract surgery has a relatively high success rate. The twenty-minute procedure is usually performed in an outpatient, same-day-surgery setting while using IV sedation. Some patients prefer general anesthesia.

Opening two satellite operations was not a simple venture. While it helped diversify my patient base, the expansion created unique challenges. For example, at my rural Somerville, Tennessee office, most of my patients were White, and for many of them, I was the first Black physician they had ever seen. It was not always love at first sight. Once, a White elderly woman completed the new patient questionnaire and sat back in her chair until I stepped in and called her back to the examination room, as I have always done in my solo practice. As we settled into the examination room, it slowly dawned on her that I was not just her escort; I was also the doctor who would treat her. A look of horror came over her face, and she refused treatment. The family members who had accompanied her could not convince her otherwise.

By this point, I was more used to the apprehension or outright refusal that afflicted some patients, and I let the experiences roll off my back more easily. I figured individuals who are racists and bigots are usually not great patients to retain in the long run anyway. They tended to be non-compliant, which often led them to ignore care instructions or prescription directions. This usually resulted in further ailments that needed treatment aligned with the current problem. It was often a frustrating back-and-forth that led nowhere. So, despite the initial insult to my skills, I figured they were doing me a favor by not allowing me to treat them.

In the meantime, Rhynette had decided on a career change of her own. She went from Memphis State University Literature professor to starting MSU Law School. Upon her graduation, we were often referred to as The Huxtables, a reference from "The Cosby Show," where Bill Cosby played a doctor, and Phylicia Rashad portrayed a lawyer in a middle-class Black American family living in Brooklyn. Interestingly, neither of us had planned to become a lawyer or a doctor after college, but we embraced our new professions. "The Huxtables" was a playful reference that made us laugh, a reflection of our journey together.

Our family was growing beautifully, too, and our second son, Ryan, was born. We found a nice house in Germantown, Tennessee. I was enthusiastic about this next chapter of our life together. However, I was less than ecstatic about being the first Black family in this upscale neighborhood. We lived on a large corner lot, about an acre and a half, that required a riding lawn mower to maintain. I enjoyed cutting my own lawn and washing my own cars. On one sunny Saturday afternoon, I was mowing my lawn sitting on a zero-turn riding mower with cool jazz blasting in my Studio Beats headphones. One of my neighbors pulled up and rolled down her car window. I thought for a moment that she might say hello and possibly introduce herself. None of our neighbors had done so up to that point. I turned off my mower and removed my headphones. Then she asked me, "How much would you charge to mow my lawn? I live right over there."

She didn't even realize I was her neighbor. In disgust, I responded: "Lady, you can't afford me."

It seemed like a never-ending cycle of racial profiling. Jokingly, I began to wonder if my neighbors had jobs themselves, as it seemed they had ample time to spend peering into my yard and wondering how a Black family could afford to live in this neighborhood. I'm sure they spent many perplexing hours conjuring up wild ideas about how we made so much money. It couldn't simply be that we were an honest, hard-working family. I'm sure they had to imagine all kinds of duplicitous things to justify their own rude behavior and harsh judgment.

Being in our neighborhood often felt like being under a microscope. Even when we could not place the stares, we felt them so clearly. It was an eerie experience to feel eyes boring into you with no one in sight, nothing but the slight wafting of window curtains setting back in place. After enduring this for a few weeks, we decided to build a brick privacy wall around one corner of our property. That's when I discovered another disadvantage of living in a lovely White neighborhood: everyone charges more for their services.

I contracted a Black masonry company, and they arrived and went to work at about the same time I was driving off to my office. I looked forward to the new addition and the privacy. But just a few hours later, I received an emergency phone call from the bricklayers. My neighbor was in a rage and claimed that they had encroached on his property by four inches. We halted construction to try to sort out the situation, but in a fortunate turn of events, the problematic neighbor decided to move away and leave the neighborhood.

One problem was gone, but this did not stop the circulating gossip about how I was earning my livelihood. Some neighbors thought I was a drug dealer, and I was inclined to let them believe whatever they wanted. If they were convinced drug dealers wore hospital scrubs to and from work, who was I to tell them otherwise? A more civil approach would have been to come by and welcome us to their neighborhood, but that only happened once.

If the neighborhood hostility was not enough, I was still being stopped by police asking what I was doing in this part of town. Despite the negative experiences with White neighbors and the occasional racial profiling, we enjoyed our Germantown home and that large lot. Eventually, I added a tennis court, a swimming pool, and a sunroom with a hot tub to the property.

It became such a nice place that a few years later, a funny thing happened. When Mike Tyson had a boxing match scheduled in Memphis, someone from his management team called and offered us an exorbitant amount of money to rent the house for a week to Mr. Tyson and his entourage. I wanted to consider it. Imagine Mike Tyson sitting at your breakfast bar. Rhynette, on the other hand, was adamantly against it, so we politely declined.

Returning to Memphis was a homecoming in many different ways, including musically. I started gigging regularly with Memphis musicians Tom Lonardo (drums), Earl Thomas (bass), and Sydney Kirk (keyboard). In the midst of the chaos that came with opening three ophthalmology offices, music became a refuge. There were long, demanding days filled with surgical cases, managing medical offices, and dealing with the interpersonal dynamics of patients and office staff. But I had nights and weekends to unwind with my bandmates: Tom on drums, Earl on bass, and Sydney on the keyboard. When we got into a groove, the stresses of the day melted away. The soothing melodies and rhythmic beats wrapped around me like a warm embrace, making the weight of any anxieties much lighter. Jam sessions felt like a breath of fresh air, a reminder that there was still calm to be found amid the hustle. We communicated through music, listening to each other play and waiting for an opening to solo or improvise. For two years, this band, called the Bill Hurd Jazz Quartet, performed every weekend at the Memphis Sounds nightclub located across the street from the famous Peabody Hotel. We also made road trips, played concerts all over the region, and developed a fanbase of jazz lovers.

Overall, it was a time of great change and excitement. I was now a doctor, and Rhynette was a corporate attorney. We had a new son and a new home. My name was literally in lights, up on the marquee over the Memphis Sounds nightclub. However, there was one downside to all the success Rhynette and I were finding in our lives: the toll it was taking on our marriage. Rhynette and I had enjoyed a storied courtship, a memorable wedding, and a blissful life in Boston as newlyweds and new parents. Over the next ten years, we both accumulated advanced degrees in different disciplines. A family friend once joked that Rhynette and I had more degrees than a thermometer.

Now, we both had our own circles of friends and colleagues,

too. The problem was these two circles rarely intersected; Rhynette would go one way, and I would head the other. We could both sense the growing disconnect, but at the same time, we were blinded by all of our success. We were a power couple. We were at the top of our game. We shared important goals, like being dedicated parents and good friends. What could go wrong?

PART V
WORLD-WIDE MISSION TRIPS

CHAPTER 15
MEDICAL MISSIONS

Some of the most meaningful experiences of my life were my medical mission trips to distant locations across several continents, which took place roughly between 1984 and the early 2000s. If you ask anyone about their participation in missionary activities, you will likely get a positive response. Whether the mission work was in New Orleans after Hurricane Katrina or in Haiti following the 2010 earthquake, what stands out is the help provided to those in need. My introduction to medical missions came during my residency at the University of Tennessee Health Science Center when Doctor Jerre Freeman led us on that eventful trip to Mexico. That trip started a love affair that would endure throughout my career. I found a deep passion for missionary work beginning with the Ometepec Project.

After Ometepec, my next mission trip took me to a small town near Santarém, Brazil, on the Amazon River, approximately three hundred miles east of Manaus. I accompanied two other Memphis eye surgeons, Doctors Thomas Gettlefinger and Ralph Hamilton,

Jr. We flew into Manaus, then took a small airplane into Santarem, a coastal city of 300,000 people where the muddy waters of the Amazon River and the clear green water of the Tapajos River visibly meet to form a breathtaking view. We performed mostly cataract surgeries, restoring sight to about 130 Brazilian patients during our week-long stay. We provided this healthcare free of charge. We wanted to ensure everyone who could visit received treatment despite a lack of funds or insurance.

Eventually, our mission trips expanded to include three large cities in China and three cities in South Africa. Unlike other trips, in China and South Africa, we saw a limited number of patients. The main goal here was to share and exchange surgical techniques and medical, diagnostic, and therapeutic procedures with the foreign host physicians. In Johannesburg, South Africa, I had the opportunity to "scrub in" on several consecutive cataract surgeries performed by a local ophthalmologist. We discussed the small differences in our techniques and approaches during each phase of the cataract surgeries. What we accomplished on these two trips was meeting and connecting with local eye surgeons and exploring what we could learn from each other.

Rhynette accompanied me on one mission trip to Ometepec, Mexico. I loved sharing the experience of travel and mission work with her, and she was a great companion. She also came with me to Johannesburg and Cape Town in South Africa as part of a larger team of Black American professionals from Memphis with the idea of exchanging strategies in the fields of medicine, law, and business.

Another memorable mission trip was to Kaolak, Senegal, a

small city of 200,000 located about one hundred forty miles east of Dakar. Alongside Doctors Lawrence Madlock and Steve Cole, both Memphians, we treated almost eight hundred patients over two and a half weeks. Blind and sick patients waited in long lines for hours after traveling from afar. The lines and hours seemed to blend together into a kind of time warp, but we didn't stop working until the last patient was seen. My trips to Africa and other underserved or underdeveloped parts of the world were perfect illustrations of why many doctors take the time away from their private practices to do medical missions: doctors see a healthcare disparity and realize they have the skills and training to meet that challenge. The next step is easy.

On one medical mission trip to West Africa, our medical team was graciously hosted by Sheik Hassan Cisse, the preeminent spokesman of the Tariqa Tijaniyya, an accomplished Islamic scholar, and the spiritual leader of millions of West Africans. The three hundred or so Senegalese patients we treated were carefully preselected and triaged before our arrival. During our stay, we were well fed, housed, and often treated like royalty. I tried to remind our hosts that we were here to help, so elaborate special treatment was not necessary. Most of the African patients our medical team treated were poor, yet they still wanted to show their gratitude by bringing food and small gifts from their homes. We did not accept these gifts but made it clear we were grateful for the kind gesture.

During our stay in Senegal, we spent an afternoon touring the House of Slaves Museum on Goree Island, a tiny island off the coast of Dakar. It is best known for its role in the Atlantic slave trade.

Goree Island is located at the westernmost tip of the African continent, providing a logistically convenient entry point to Africa for the European slave ships that came from the north. It has been estimated more than 20 million West African men, women, and children were bought and taken against their will, beginning with the Portuguese in the early 1500s and expanding for three centuries. Standing in the center of one of the slave houses, I was overcome with an indescribably eerie feeling, knowing that some of my own African ancestors had probably passed through these very walls, bound painfully in connecting chains and shackles.

Several years later, on a busy day back in my Memphis office, I received a surprising phone call. My assistant interrupted me with apologies and informed me that an unusual caller was holding the line for me. "Who is it?" I asked.

"A representative for Sheik Hassan Cisse?" She replied with some apprehension. I guess it's not every day a West African sheik dials up a Memphis doctor's office.

I was thrilled to hear from him, though, and his representatives informed me that Sheik Cisse was in Memphis and wished to have his eyes examined. "Of course," I said without hesitation. I asked my staff to kindly reschedule my afternoon appointments, and we cleared out the waiting room to accommodate Sheik Cisse and his entourage. I remembered well the royal and gracious care that our medical team had received from this esteemed West African spiritual leader. It was important to me to honor the customs and culture of African religious royalty by showing the utmost respect in return.

CHAPTER 16
MADAGASCAR

Our medical mission trips to Madagascar hold a special place in my heart for a few reasons, but one of those was that we pioneered these events from start to finish. These weren't occasions where we were invited to join a previously existing program; we built the program to go and meet a need. In another case of worlds colliding, these medical mission trips came about in response to a request by Lee Evans. Lee Evans was the 400-meter Olympic gold medalist and former world record holder at the Olympic Games in Mexico City in 1968. We were longtime friends and former collegiate track competitors.

Each year, the NCAA presents the Silver Anniversary Award to six former student-athletes who were All-Americans in their sport, graduated 25 years earlier, and made significant societal contributions. In 1994, 25 years after my Notre Dame graduation, the NCAA honored Kareem Abdul-Jabbar (UCLA), Calvin Hill (Yale), Jim Ryun (Kansas), Leroy Keyes (Purdue), Lee Evans (San Jose State), and me with this prestigious award. All of us had achieved All-American status in 1969 and had made notable contributions to our communities. I believe my selection was largely due to my medical mission work, particularly in Africa.

The notification was a delightful surprise. While I was seeing patients at one of my clinics, I received a call from Willie White, a five-time Olympian (1956–1972) and member of the NCAA Silver Anniversary selection committee. When she listed names like Kareem Abdul-Jabbar, Jim Ryun, and Calvin Hill and then included me, I questioned whether she had the right William Hurd. She responded that I was one of the easier choices. While I have received many awards since my time at Notre Dame, the 1994 NCAA Silver Anniversary Award remains one of my most treasured honors.

This NCAA ceremony was held in San Antonio, Texas, and broadcast on CNN. Lee and I talked after the program, and he convinced me that I should bring a medical team to Antananarivo, Madagascar, where he was living at the time, with his wife, who was Malagasy or Madagascan. After months of planning, and with help from Ambassador Shirley Barnes, then the US Ambassador to Madagascar (1998–2001), Doctor Madlock, Doctor Cole, and I traveled to Madagascar. Prior to our arrival, Ms. Barnes had facilitated the timely delivery and clearance through customs of a freight-size container full of medical supplies and equipment donated by the VA Hospital and local Memphis pharmacies. Alcon and Bausch and Lomb (B&L) donated significant numbers of intraocular lenses and other surgical supplies needed for performing cataract surgeries. As usual on surgical mission trips, I brought my personal surgical instruments and magnifying loupes to use in place of a large bulky operating microscope.

Madagascar is the earth's fourth largest island, located off the southeast coast of Africa, separated from the continent by the Mozambique Channel. In January 2000—summertime in Madagascar and the end of the rainy season—an entourage of officials from USAID and SALVA, along with Lee Evans and his wife and children, met Steve Cole, Lawrence Madlock, and me at the airport in Antananarivo, the capital city of Madagascar. On the second day, we were flown to the northeast coastal city of Sambava, then traveled by car about 110 miles north to another coastal town, Vohimar, which was a remote, rural, and almost bush-like town with a population of 10,000.

In Vohemar, in a small hospital with two local physicians and a surgeon, I prepped my station, including microsurgical instruments, magnifying loupes, a stack of donated intraocular lenses (IOLs), viscoelastics, 10-0 nylon sutures, and other surgical supplies required for cataract surgery. After screening about 225 patients the first morning, I started operating that afternoon. I was prepared, much like during other mission trips, to work until the wee hours of the night until every patient was seen.

I saw several cases of advanced undiagnosed glaucoma. Glaucoma is a blinding eye condition usually requiring lifelong treatment to maintain a normal range of intraocular pressure (IOP), mostly by using eye pressure-lowering eye drops or laser and minimally invasive surgical procedures to create an outflow pathway of aqueous humor, the clear liquid inside the front part of the eye. The only medication in the hospital for glaucoma was Acetazolamide (250mg tablets), which was prescribed twice a day for two weeks and then discontinued—obviously not a very effective way to treat this serious eye condition. Unfortunately, these glaucoma patients could not afford to buy even the least expensive effective eye drops, a very sad situation. As a result, I performed a dozen or so surgical trabeculectomies (a surgical filtering procedure aimed at lowering the intraocular pressure by creating a small opening inside the eye at the trabecular meshwork), especially on younger patients with advanced glaucoma and severe optic nerve cupping.

Unfortunately, I had to limit cataract surgery to the worst-seeing eye in those patients with bilateral hypermature or advanced cataracts in both eyes. I performed strabismus surgery on younger patients with crossed or misaligned eyes who had no amblyopia (or very poor vision or no vision). The local surgeon often assisted me when he was not busy. He seemed fascinated to see eye surgery performed in his hospital for the first time.

Doctors Steve Cole and Lawrence Madlock treated patients with the two general local doctors, resulting in a healthy exchange of Western and Third-World clinical practice. Patients had traveled from all over the countryside to see us, the American doctors, and wanted to be cured of their illnesses. Even though we did not expect anything in return for our services, some patients still wanted to show their gratitude with fascinating gifts.

After four days in Vohemar, we traveled back to Sambava, passing through many small villages, often stopping to allow herds of cattle, sheep, or wild horses to cross. This was an unusual yet beautiful sight. The land was vast here, full of lush green plants, unusual trees, and rain forests. The mountains, coastlines, and beaches were breathtaking. We spent the next six days in Antananarivo, the capital city, where I worked with Dr. Jeannine Rambohanta, one of only three ophthalmologists in all of Madagascar. Having no access to an operating microscope, once again, cataract surgery was limited to severe cases. Before leaving Madagascar, I left the remaining surgical supplies, including my cherished magnifying ocular loupes, to aid Dr. Rambohanta, a skilled and capable eye surgeon.

On a second trip to Madagascar, we saw more than 1,200 patients, and I performed about 40 surgery cases, mostly cataracts. This was when I met the colorfully dressed, stoic grandmother with the mature bilateral cataracts who had never seen her toddler granddaughter. This was the moment we both cried after I removed the gauze covering the eye that I had operated on the previous day. When she opened her eyes, she could see clearly for the first time in two years. I could write chapters about the unique, unforgettable experiences of our world mission trips and how lives were changed or improved—including ours. A full account of my last Madagascar mission trip was written for the monthly medical journal *Ophthalmology Times* in a January 2000 article titled "Medical Mission."

I am deeply honored and humbled to have had a place in healing sick patients. Making medicine more accessible was all I hoped to achieve when I decided to attend medical school. I swore to myself that I would be patient, kind, and, most importantly, treat my patients with dignity. These trips will forever be some of my most significant and life-enriching experiences. Eventually, I had to cease my medical missions because of the logistical difficulties and safety issues surrounding these trips and because of my personal health.

In the spring of 2000, I went for a routine office visit to my friend and urologist, Dr. Charles Wallace. Both of our medical practices were in the same office building on the campus of Methodist University Hospital. My office was on the second floor, and his on the fifth floor. As part of a routine urological office visit, a blood specimen was taken to determine my prostate-specific antigen (PSA). Several days passed before the result came back from the lab. Then, Dr. Wallace summoned me back to his office with the surprising news that my PSA had risen to 6.5 when the normal range was 0 to 4.0. He wanted to perform a prostate biopsy immediately to determine if I had prostate cancer. Anxious to know if I actually had cancer or a less serious condition called prostatitis (inflammation or infection of the prostate gland), I agreed and allowed Dr. Wallace to perform a prostate biopsy right then and there in his office without anesthesia. I got into position on an exam table in his office treatment room, and he took out his sterile instruments and proceeded.

The procedure was fairly painful, and I bled. I didn't regret having it done so quickly because I was anxious to know the results, but I swore I would never do anything like that again without anesthesia, and I live by those words to this day.

The biopsy came back positive for Stage I prostate cancer,

but fortunately, it was not the aggressive form of the disease. With this cancer diagnosis, I initially fell into a depression and began to think about my mortality in a whole new way. Up until now, I had simply been too busy to die. But I had to think about things differently now. I also had to decide my source of treatment. Robotic prostatectomy had not yet evolved in 2000, so I opted for brachytherapy (or radioactive seed implants) plus external beam radiation. In the operating room, the brachytherapy required a physicist, a radiologist/oncologist, and a urologist to ensure the precise placement of the radioactive seed implants around the prostate cancer cells.

After accepting my cancer diagnosis and getting treatment, I began to share my story with family and friends and encouraged the men in my life to get PSA tests regularly. Being a physician, I know the importance of early detection of diseases. I remember sharing my story with the members of the Add-In Tennis Club shortly after my diagnosis. I told them that prostate cancer is 3 to 4 times more common in Black men over forty and is a leading cause of death if untreated. But most importantly, it can't be treated if it's not diagnosed. I became a spokesman of sorts for early diagnosis and treatment of prostate cancer, especially in Black men.

My subclinical depression was short-lived as I started to realize how grateful I was to be in a position to help others—not to mention being able to put a smile on someone's face while they listened to the music from my saxophone. People close to me don't like hearing me say this, but I am no longer afraid of death. I hope that my life can, in some small way, serve as inspiration and help people see that it is okay to help your neighbor or fellow man, especially the less fortunate.

It has now been almost twenty-five years since my prostate cancer diagnosis, and I am still alive and well. As a physician, I know that the probability of my cancer returning is greater than zero. As a patient, I have the right peace of mind that I will cross that bridge when I get to it.

PART VI
RETIREMENT

CHAPTER 17

THE END IS JUST THE BEGINNING

In August 2019, I retired from private practice after thirty-six fulfilling years managing a solo ophthalmology office. A few factors drove the decision to retire: my declining health, the cumulative stress of managing a private practice, and other personal considerations. It was clear that the demands of my career were taking a toll on me. At this stage in my life, I felt a strong need to begin reflecting on my journey—beyond all the accomplishments, awards, and honors. I came into a period of introspection. My goal was to eliminate stress and drama, accept past mistakes, and learn from them. This process, almost like meditation, put me on a mission to better myself. Although still a work in progress, the results have been very positive. I've found greater peace of mind and am in a better place concurrent with my retirement.

I truly enjoyed my profession and derived great satisfaction from engaging with patients, restoring sight for many, and working with so many other talented physicians. The thing I miss the most is the operating room, however. Performing surgeries was like running a race or playing a jazz solo; it was the moment when all my skill, experience, and concentration came together to achieve a singular goal. In the operating suite, I felt at ease and confident; this was my comfort zone. To help relax my patients, I often played soothing jazz music during surgeries, sometimes even my own compositions. I was careful to remain humble, always showing respect to the O.R. nurses, who truly run the show.

Throughout my career, I participated in numerous community health fairs, serving a population that often felt invisible. Many of my patients were uninsured, low-income individuals or those who had been turned away by other ophthalmologists. People often questioned my choice to help these underserved communities, but for me, the answer was simple: where else would they go? Rather than focusing on what I might be giving up by providing care to underprivileged people, I appreciated all there was to gain. Some might argue I was sacrificing money or time, arguably the most precious currency, but I always found a way to treat one more patient. One more patient wouldn't change my life drastically, but the care I offered might just change that person's life.

This is work I am able to continue even now, after retirement. Although I no longer perform surgeries, I still see patients with significant medical problems at a community health center where my focus remains on eye exams for those without insurance, often low-income individuals, including many post-incarcerated and homeless patients. I go to this clinic just half a day a week to keep my medical license active, yet in that short time, I encounter so many people in need—and a wide range of pathology.

I try to take full advantage of this new role to help others. Often, I see Black men come in with extremely high blood pressure readings or diabetics with A1C levels at 13.5%. These moments lead to tough conversations, but I'm now in a position to take the time with these patients to explain some hard truths about poorly controlled diabetes. Without significant changes to diet and overall improvement in diabetic management, there are severe consequences: blindness, the need for kidney dialysis, and even amputation of a foot or leg. Taking these extra moments, it is possible to improve their long-term outcomes, not just treat the symptoms of the day or just write a prescription for eyeglasses. It is interesting that my clinical demographic data show that the group with the lowest levels of proactivity and patient compliance is Black males. Accordingly, I try to make them more conscious of their own health.

My own health continues to be a challenge, too. In 2019, I faced a setback in my battle against prostate cancer. My prostate-specific antigen (PSA) levels began to rise rapidly over an eight-month period, reaching a startling high of 74. For context, a normal PSA level ranges from 0 to 4, and mine had never previously exceeded 13.

To investigate, my urologist Dr. Rayford ordered a PET scan and an MRI to check for potential metastasis of my prostate cancer to my bones or other organs. The PET scan came back negative for bone metastasis, but the MRI revealed the involvement of the pelvic lymph nodes. Consequently, I was prescribed Xtandi, a relatively new medication for patients with advanced prostate cancer. Xtandi, though costly at $40 per pill, was made affordable through Pfizer's patient assistance program, allowing me to avoid the $160 daily expense. Xtandi functions by further reducing serum testosterone through a different mechanism than the Lupron injections I had been receiving every six months. The treatment has been remarkably effective for me. Over the past five years, my PSA levels have dropped dramatically from a high of 74 to a near-undetectable level of 0.01.

There are many joys of being retired, too. I no longer worry about payroll taxes, liability insurance, or declining office revenue. Instead, I can now immerse myself in various hobbies, including my first love: music. Golf, travel, and community involvement also enrich my life, but music remains at the forefront of my passions. I've dedicated significant time to becoming a more skilled musician, with daily practice sessions sometimes extending for hours.

As any professional saxophonist would appreciate, I strive to achieve a harmonic sound that is both lyrical and uniquely my own. This characteristic sound and tone come from extensive listening to other musicians and countless hours of practice. For aspiring saxophonists aiming to improve their sound, start first with the reed and ligature setup. Next, experiment with different mouthpieces. Finally, invest in a professional-grade horn to take your sound to the next level.

When I perform at gigs now, my fellow musicians often notice the maturation of my tone, which is one of the highest compliments a musician can receive. Spending four to five hours a day practicing and listening to music feels more like a rewarding journey than a mundane task.

My gigging schedule is now comfortably manageable, avoiding the regular weekend nightclub commitments. Locally, I frequently perform at The Mahogany, a Black-owned restaurant, alongside some of my favorite fellow musicians: Audie Smith on keyboards, Reggie Tabor on drums, and Vince Oglesby on bass. Our band performs at many Memphis venues and events, including the Germantown Performing Arts Center, Crosstown Arts, the Ben Hooks Central Library, and Sunset Jazz at Court Square in downtown Memphis.

I continue to collaborate with Charles Curl in Hilton Head, South Carolina, two or three times a year to work on albums and musical projects in his state-of-the-art home studio. We have recorded three albums in Curl's studio: *Magic Music*, *Hip Pocket*, and *Return of the Hip*, which has been critically acclaimed and is available on Spotify and other streaming services under the title "Curl and Hurd."

My second hobby is playing golf. More than just the game, I love the comradery established among golfing buddies and the interesting people you meet on the golf course. I have introduced the game to some of my closest friends, and it provides us with another way to connect and spend time together. Louis Taylor, from St. Thomas, U.S., Virgin Islands, is one of those friends. He was the keyboardist with our jazz band during my time in Nashville while he was a student at Tennessee State University. I was on one of my frequent trips to St. Thomas to perform with Louis and his Caribbean jazz band when he challenged me to a game, even though I was the one who introduced it to him. On this particular trip, I didn't bring my golf clubs, only two saxophones, and my luggage. He insisted we play anyhow so he could show off his improved golfing skills, so I rented a set of TaylorMade clubs from the clubhouse at the Mahogany Run Golf course in St Thomas. This is a beautiful course, and several holes have spectacular ocean views. On the twelfth hole, a par three, 120-yard downhill, I recorded a hole-in-one using a nine iron rental club, a feat which I often remind Louis of. With a lot of luck and a bit of skill, I have made four holes-in-one over time. Even the memories of those shots provide a lot of joy and satisfaction. Some golfers play a lifetime and never have a single hole-in-one.

CHAPTER 18

NOTRE DAME RECONNECTIONS

My post-retirement travel schedule has included trips back to the Notre Dame campus. At reunions and alumni events, I am frequently reminded of the positive impressions I made as an athlete, a student, and a musician. Although I didn't experience blatant racism at Notre Dame, I was one of the very few Black students, so the impressions I made on people were often enduring, especially since they were made at a time when the nation was experiencing huge racial and social upheavals. I believe I contributed in my small way to positively changing the perception that some people held of Black students and athletes.

And now, decades later, it's a delight to be invited back to campus. Larry Dwyer, class of '66 was the trombonist and leader of an award-winning Jazz Sextet that I was also a member of. He is currently Assistant Director of Bands and Director of Jazz Studies at Notre Dame. Larry has invited me to be a regular visiting guest artist in one of his Jazz Studies classes. These scheduled campus visits provide an opportunity to reconnect with Notre Dame classmates and close friends in South Bend, Indiana. Two of my track teammates live in South Bend and continue to be dear and close friends. Dr. Mark Walsh, a brilliant and multi-talented Emergency Room physician, has done enormous work during volunteer medical missions in Haiti. Dan Saracino was an assistant provost for enrollment at Notre Dame.

Dr. Mark Walsh and Dan Saracino in a playful moment

Mark once invited me to his Washington, D.C. home to meet his Italian mother when the Notre Dame track team competed in an indoor track meet in the D.C. area in late 1968. Similarly, when a few members of the track team had qualified for an invitational outdoor track meet in San Diego, California, Dan invited me into his home to meet his father. Men like Mark, Dan, Ole Skarstein, Bob

Timm, Pete Farrell, Ken Howard, Ed Broderick and Doug Breunlin made my college experience memorable. We practiced, traveled, and competed together—and we are now lifelong friends.

Being a well-known and record-holding Notre Dame athlete, many classmates who I never knew very well or at all, knew about me. As a freshman, students knew where I was from, my fastest time in the one-hundred-yard dash, my GPA, and even my SAT scores. One such guy was Eddie Fitzpatrick. Fast forward to forty-five years later, I got a phone call from Eddie, introducing himself as a former classmate who followed my career. He wanted to invite me to play in a four-person golf scramble at Notre Dame's beautiful new Warren Golf Course. I gladly accepted his invitation. The golf event raised funds for the Mike McCoy Ministries. Standing 6'5" and weighing 275 pounds, Mike was an All-American defensive tackle who went on to have a brilliant NFL career. That golf event was the beginning of several more outings with Eddie and, more significantly, a friendship that had no chance to develop while we were students.

Eddie now lives in San Diego, and in 2018, the Notre Dame football team traveled to San Diego to Play Navy (and defeat them 44-22). Eddie saw this football game as an opportunity to bring me out to the West Coast and have me perform at Dizzy's Jazz Club, a San Diego venue founded by a notable Notre Dame alum, Chuck Perrin. I remembered Chuck Perrin from the days when he played his guitar and sang folk songs at a South Bend coffee house near campus in the late '60s. He named Dizzy's after the famous jazz trumpeter Dizzy Gillespie.

I flew into L.A. from Memphis, rented a car, visited my son

Ryan and his wife Priscilla in Santa Monica, and then drove to San Diego. Chuck had arranged for me to perform with three local jazz musicians: a pianist, an upright bassist, and a drummer. I arrived early enough to have a good, strong rehearsal, demonstrating once again the power of music and the ease with which total strangers communicate while playing music together.

As the crowd poured into Dizzy's that Friday evening, I was told that there were two bus-loads of people from the Notre Dame Club of San Diego, plus fans attending the ND-Navy game the next day. The atmosphere was electric, and it showed in our performance as the impromptu band had a blast playing together. I purposely selected a song list of recognizable contemporary and pop tunes and added plenty of jazz improvisation. After our performance, several people came up and said it was one of the best jazz concerts they had attended. It could be that, for some, this was the *first* jazz concert they had attended, but still, we had a ball.

I stayed at Eddie's house for the night. He has a beautiful contemporary-style home in an elevated suburb overlooking San Diego. We stayed up late talking over several glasses of merlot. For one moment, the conversation turned to politics, and for the first time in our friendship, we found ourselves on opposite sides of the equation. Eddie quickly suggested we stop talking about politics, and I agreed. We had too many positive things to connect over.

Eddie and I talk often. He is currently suffering from Parkinson's disease. We reach out to each other routinely, and I always look forward to another visit on one of my West Coast ventures.

CHAPTER 19
FAMILY PRIDE AND SORROW

Another great gift of retirement is the ability to focus more on family and spend time with the ones we love. From this vantage point, I can truly appreciate the journey that we have made together, take pride in my children, and enjoy the energy and accomplishments of the younger generations. My older sister, Avar H. James, attended LeMoyne-Owen College in Memphis, our father's alma mater. She published her first book, *Following His Lead*, a collection of religious poems, and is currently working on her second book. Avar is married to Bill James. Bill is a tall, handsome and engaging gentleman who, like me, is a lover of fine automobiles. He has the largest collection of Cole Haan shoes I have ever seen. They lived briefly in Anchorage, Alaska, before settling in Maryville, Tennessee, just outside Knoxville, where they raised three children: Will (Pooka), Chris, and Ashley.

My sisters, Avar and Mildred, and me

Charles Russell Branham, the brother of the Branham twins, graduated from Manassas High School in 1963 and Rockford College in 1967, where he served as student body president and was inducted into Phi Beta Kappa. Dr. Branham also enjoyed a distinguished career as a history professor at the University of Chicago. In addition, he held the position of senior historian at the famous DuSable Black History Museum in Chicago. I am very proud to be his first cousin.

My cousin, Dr. Charles R. Branham Souce: The Historymakers

My two sons have been such a source of pride and joy for me for so many years that I barely have words to describe it.

Bill Jr. is outgoing, confident, and naturally talented in many areas. He didn't study as much as I did, but he was so naturally gifted that success in academics came without a lot of effort. He completed graduate study in Healthcare Administration at the University of Memphis. When he started looking for employment, he had many choices before him. He chose to join me in my private practice, even though working at a hospital would have paid him twice as much. I was touched and honored by his decision and loved working with him for many years. He became the manager of my office optical dispensary shop. I was often reminded of the time when he was a boy; I overheard him tell his friends that he wanted to be just like his father. Now, here we were, working together. We enjoy each other's company at the office or on the golf course.

My younger son, Ryan, is nine years younger than Bill Jr., so their sibling bonding didn't really develop until adulthood. Unlike Bill Jr., Ryan was more reserved, deeply focused, and studious—a true "nerd," much like myself. Also like me, he attended Notre Dame, where he came out of his shell and became quite popular. I'll never forget the moment he introduced me at a speaking event on campus where I was invited to deliver an Emil T Hoffman lecture in October of 2000. Ryan was just a freshman, and this was the first time I ever heard him speak in front of an audience. I was struck by his poise and articulation. I was moved almost to tears by his introduction and had to quickly compose myself before taking the podium to deliver my lecture.

Ryan graduated from Notre Dame in 2005 with honors, having completed a double major in Japanese and computer science. He was also a Monogram winner during his last two years, lettering in track & field and earning a scholarship that covered his tuition, room, and board. This was money-saving for me. After earning his master's degree from Savannah College of Art and Design (SCAD), he worked in Toronto, Beijing, and Tokyo for four years. While teaching in Beijing, Ryan was assigned a personal interpreter, an attractive Chinese woman named Priscilla, who eventually became his wife. Rhynette conducted their wedding ceremony in her judicial chambers. Ryan now has his dream job in L.A. as a visual effects artist and computer animator. His wife Priscilla recently earned her doctorate from U.C.L.A. and is now a college professor.

My son Ryan and his wife, Priscilla

Madison is my first grandchild. I remember tutoring her in her ninth-grade math course, as she needed someone to make math more interesting and useful. When she enrolled at the University of Memphis, I bought her first car, a VW Jetta. She could then go back and forth to class without depending on others. Madison is now enrolled in the Aviation program at U of M and has recently earned her student pilot license. I am sure she now enjoys using mathematics to delineate the principles of aviation. She gets special love and support from Rhynette. Madison's other grandfather, Stanley McKinney, and I have become close friends.

My nephew Chris James, who now lives in Los Angeles with his wife, Robyn, has an impressive musical career. He has worked with Michael Jackson, toured with Prince, and played keyboards on Luther Vandross' *Dance with My Father* album. Chris is a two-time Grammy nominee for his work as a music studio engineer. Chris's brother Will, aka Pooka, also based in L.A., is an executive at Kia Automotives and is married to Ailene. They have two beautiful, tall, and athletic daughters. Pooka, Bill Jr and I golf whenever possible. My niece Ashley is the sister of Chris and Pooka. She has a son Ashton who is a UT freshman and up and coming saxophonist. I recently gifted him one of my soprano saxophones. Ashley also has a lovely 10 year old daughter named Brooklyn.

My 15-year-old grandson Carson's drive for competitive swimming brings back fond memories of my own passion for track and field. During the school year, I often pick him up from the University Campus School, where he's a sophomore, and take him to his swimming practice. His excitement to get into the practice pool and his aversion to being late remind me of my own commitment to sports. Carson is also shining academically. Instead of splurging on the latest pair of Jordan Nike shoes, I opted to reward him with fifty dollars for every A he earns on his report card. He impressed me with five A's, the majority of which came from Advanced Placement courses. When I shared this with Rhynette, she suggested offering double rewards for the AP A's, and I'm more than happy to invest in his success. Carson currently has a part-time job as a lifeguard at a local athletic center and is now contemplating his future in competitive swimming as a collegiate student athlete.

My grandson Carson and my granddaughter Madison

Of course, every family has its struggles, too, and not all of my family visits have been joyful ones. My only brother, Leon Jr., attended Wilberforce University in Ohio and spent most of his professional career as an accountant in Washington, D.C. Despite no family history of cardiovascular disease, Leon had to undergo open-heart surgery to replace a faulty heart valve while still in D.C. I went there to support him through the surgery.

After a lengthy family discussion, I flew back to D.C., and Leon and I packed all his valuable belongings into his Volvo sedan. We drove the car back to Memphis, where Leon would live with our aging mother, who had been living alone.

My brother, Leon Jr.

Leon Jr. had some quirky mannerisms and idiosyncrasies that even our dad noticed early on. Despite these traits, I loved my brother dearly and would do anything for him. We shared many brotherly moments, and although he was older, he often sought my advice and support. At one point, he even tried to give me advice on my marital problems despite having been married and divorced four times himself. I told him, "Hey man, get the heck outta here." We ended up laughing so hard it hurt.

In 2018, I was at Leon's hospital bedside just before he was taken in for surgery to repair a dissecting aortic aneurysm. Unfortunately, he did not survive the twelve-hour cardiac operation, which was performed by two of Memphis' top cardiac surgeons whom I knew well. Like my father before him, we lost Leon Jr. too soon.

I've always believed in second chances, and I try to give everyone the benefit of the doubt. When I taught at Tennessee State

University, I rarely failed anyone. If a student showed me effort, time, and dedication, I was willing to go the extra mile to help them improve. My father used to say, "Give them an E for effort," and that mantra has stuck with me throughout my life.

My sister Mildred is also someone who inspires me to look for the good in everyone, as she did when she struggled with her daughter, Mia, in the wake of Mildred's husband's (George Langston) death. Her daughter, Mia, struggled with addiction for years. Mia's history with drugs was long and painful, marked by a cycle of rehab stints that promised hope but often ended in relapse. Mia was also in and out of church as she often requested to be baptized again. She dealt with many other life challenges as well. For a brief period, Mia even worked in my office as an insurance clerk, but her addiction took a darker turn, and she left my employment. One has to be reminded that drug addiction is a disease much like diabetes or cancer or mental disorder and the consequences of inadequate treatment can be fatal.

Through it all, her mother, Mildred, remained unwaveringly supportive, constantly reaching out to help Mia, who fought hard to regain her health. After several stints in rehab, she lost a significant amount of extra weight and looked vibrant, leading everyone to believe she had finally turned a corner. But that hope was short-lived. She soon fell back into the clutches of addiction. Compounding her struggles, Mia became involved with a man who shared her addiction, and their relationship took a violent turn when he struck her, injuring her eye so severely that she ultimately lost it.

Mia also voluntarily gave custody of her son, Caleb, who, despite her deep love for him, was ultimately taken in by her mother, Mildred, as legal guardian during Mia's darkest times. She died in 2023 when she was only in her early forties.

Mia's journey was marked by loss and resilience. Her story might sound familiar to many, yet every family's struggle with drug addiction is solely their own, never to be replicated in another. It is difficult to speak of Mia without feeling a range of emotions from guilt to utter sadness, but I hope that by sharing my own family's struggle, others will feel comfort in their own. Many people have family members who suffer from drug or alcohol addiction, and the impacts are felt far and wide, both financially and emotionally.

CHAPTER 20
WHAT IF

Retirement allows plenty of time to think about the "What ifs" and the mistakes of the past that continue to haunt me. One of my major "What ifs" is my father dying before he could see everything I accomplished. My father was my greatest inspiration. As a child, I looked up to him more than anyone else; he was the benchmark for the man I wanted to become. My heart aches with the regret that he never got to witness my journey to becoming a doctor. I know he would have beamed with pride, and the thought that he'll never know I completed medical school weighs heavily on me. He loved to share stories of my achievements with everyone he met, from friends to strangers on the street. And I loved to share with him.

In everyone's life, there are failures for which we are responsible. My biggest failure is marriage. I was proud of being many things in life: a great provider, father, son, brother, and friend. But I was not always a great husband. There are many "What ifs" when I think back over the years. It is hard for me to discuss this, as I feel regret for some of my decisions as a younger man. I realize I am no longer that person, but whether I am or not, it does not take away the stress and pain I put Rhynette through during the decades of our marriage. In many ways, she is everything you would want in a life partner: a great friend, wife, and mother. Perhaps I was young and moving too fast. I wanted to achieve everything within my grasp, but I never stopped to wonder why I was grasping for it. I became greedy for achievements, and my marriage suffered from a lack of communication and openness. It was no surprise then that Rhynette and I eventually decided to separate our lives.

Talking about our marital discord is difficult for me, but I think it is appropriate to share in this memoir. I want to show that with all of the gifts I have been blessed with, I have imperfections. First of all, I take full responsibility for our marriage problems. I know I messed up. I cannot undo the past, but I can learn from my mistakes and ask for forgiveness.

Rhynette and I sought help by attending several sessions of marriage counseling. In one of the earlier sessions, it became apparent to me that the male therapist was more interested in flirting with Rhynette rather than counseling us on our marriage. I was torn between feeling jealous of another man flirting with my attractive wife or feeling disgusted that a professional therapist would behave so inappropriately.

We switched counselors. Looking back, I am convinced that more sessions with a professional marriage counselor would have been beneficial for Rhynette and me, but at the time, we didn't see the value in it. Now, that's another "What if" I live with.

I miss seeing and being with her daily, and I still love her, but I understand that some things cannot be overlooked or forgotten. I can only move forward with the promise to myself to never be the husband or person I once was ever again.

Telling our sons was a reflection of their personalities. My first son saw the writing on the wall years ago and was unsurprised by this announcement. My second son, Ryan, who is more reserved and quiet, respected our decision but had little to say on the matter. I hope to have more in-depth conversations with them about the separation to check on the emotional effect it may have had. I've learned over the years that emotional stoicism is not always the best state of mind for mental health and stability.

As I get older, there are other "What ifs" related to close friends and family members suffering from geriatric illness, disease, and cancer. *What if they had done something differently? What if I had done more when I had the chance?* I decided that I would not miss any opportunities to connect with these loved ones while I still had time to do so.

My Aunt Johnice Parker was my mother's sister, living in Dallas. She is a supremely gifted artist. Johnice had been calling me frequently, her voice growing faint and her speech incoherent as she succumbed to liver cancer. I visited her shortly before her passing. Johnice's mother, Ruth Ingram Parker, was also the mother of renowned saxophonist Charles Lloyd.

I also made a trip to see my dear friend Walter King in Nashville. Walter, the nephew of, and eventual musical director and arranger for B.B. King, was battling advanced type I diabetes and its complications. He had already lost eyesight in his right eye from diabetic retinopathy, was on kidney dialysis from diabetic nephropathy and had his left big toe amputated from diabetic neuropathy. He had been calling me almost weekly, reminiscing about the jazz band we had in Nashville during my time at Meharry Medical College. Like Johnice's calls, Walter's frequent communication made me suspect that something was wrong.

After one of Walter's tri-weekly kidney dialysis treatments, he called to express how much he valued our long friendship and our musical collaboration in the 1970s. The next day, I got in my car and drove the 200 miles to Nashville to spend half a day with him. His wife, Brenda, prepared a light snack as we reminisced, laughed, and played his extensive collection of saxophones. Walter King passed away a few weeks later.

At times, I did not realize the full impact my friendship has had on others. For example, two days after my mother died, I got a phone call from a former patient, Mrs. Bessie Forte. Her husband, Eddie, and I were musical friends and would always talk about saxophones during her quarterly office visits. Her phone call was succinct and depressing. Eddie had just died. But before he died, he told her he wanted me to have his coveted, vintage five-digit Selmer Mark VI tenor saxophone. I played this sax on gigs for a year or so and would always proudly acknowledge how it came into my possession.

A year later, however, a Forte family member called to inform me that Eddie's vintage saxophone needed to be returned to the Forte family. Without hesitation, I returned the sax immediately because I did not want to be the source of any family drama. Even though I was only able to keep the saxophone for about a year, I cherish the time I had as a testament to my friendship with Eddie.

Reflecting on my high school experience in Memphis, I think back to the twelve segregated Black high schools of the 1950s and 60s and often wonder what could have been achieved if we had access to tennis or golf teams. How many potential Serena Williams or Tiger Woods fell victim to the harsh realities of racism and a lack of opportunity?

The weight of the problems of the world is often heavy, so I want to be aware but not consumed. I purposely stepped back and avoided political, religious, and social discussions, as I felt that opposing viewpoints on these topics rarely come together. They became just another source of stress and anxiety, and I had too much of that already. Much of that stress was self-induced, maintaining a medical career, gigging on weekends, playing golf and tennis, and trying to find time for family life.

I believe the three ophthalmology offices were the primary source of my anxiety, however. As a doctor performing multiple surgeries daily, I had a lot of patients to care about and follow up with. I wanted all of them to be comfortable and safe, and while I had confidence in my abilities, the concern for their recovery weighed heavily on me. I gave my patients my personal number after surgery, encouraging them to reach out with any questions or concerns. I received many calls, but I was always happy to respond. And despite the stress, my office and the operating room were always my happy place. I created a calming environment that allowed me to do really enjoyable service to the best of my ability so that my patients have the best possible outcome.

The business side of medicine was also where a lot of stress originated. Managing accounts, dealing with liability insurance, and handling payroll were challenging, especially in a private practice. In the last three years, I had to reduce my hours due to a bad knee, which led to a decline in office revenue.

Looking back, I realize I should have closed my practice a few years earlier. My patients felt like family, and I hated the thought of disappointing them, so I pushed myself to continue longer than my body intended. Letting my staff go was particularly difficult; I've always struggled with firing people. This time, however, I was saying goodbye to a significant chapter of my life, too. The time had come for me to leave my beloved business.

Over the last few years, I have finally reached a point in my life where my stress levels are manageable, and I've found some peace of mind. This period allowed me to rediscover myself through self-reflection and written words. I have grown to recognize and accept there are some aspects of my journey that have not been resolved and probably will never be. Racism has permeated my life like an ugly and metastatic cancer. Although facing racist behavior has made me stronger, over time, I have become less tolerant and more impatient when confronted with it. Experience has taught me not to bet money that a racist can ever be converted to a non-racist. I have this far-fetched notion and hope that racist ideology and behavior can be treated like an illness. As a scientific thinker, I envision this as requiring an analytical approach where socio-pathological behavior is first quantified. Then, the result of this complex measurement is fed back into an algorithm that, in turn, inhibits negative social behavior, much like a negative feedback system. It all sounds far-fetched and over-simplified, but this is one of the new "equations" I think about, like in the old days when I would work on math problems from the MIT magazine.

I am often asked to speak to young, underprivileged Black male students these days, also. In doing so, I often find some common denominators: a lack of motivation, little hope for the future, and no real-life, living role models. It makes me so thankful I had *all* those things growing up. At the end of these informal talks, there are usually one or two students out of about twenty-five or thirty young men who come up to me, eager to absorb any advice I have on becoming successful, and I offer it freely. Success is relative, but to most people, it simply means being happy and able to support yourself and your family financially. I have been blessed to be able to do both of those things, and it is a joy to help others do the same in whatever small way I can.

EPILOGUE

I began writing this memoir during the COVID-19 pandemic. Being cooped up at home left me with so much time on my hands that I decided to start reading. As a child, I rarely picked up fiction novels or memoirs; I always preferred mathematics or science books. Years later, Rhynette would jokingly call me illiterate for my lack of interest in literature beyond the *American Journal of Ophthalmology* or one of its peers. However, during the pandemic, I immersed myself in three inspiring memoirs: Trevor Noah's *Born a Crime*, Viola Davis's *Finding Me*, and Debra Lee's *I Am Debra Lee*. In a matter of days, I quickly read all three books. These stories inspired me in many ways, but the most surprising was that I found myself wanting to write. Seeing how these admirable people put their own experiences into writing and provided such perspective and insights made me look back and examine my own life in a way I never had before. I decided to share my story and add my voice to the great narrative of Life in America.

I wanted people to understand how fortunate I was to have the opportunity to explore and nurture my gifts. I made the most of my chances, recognizing that not everyone is afforded the same opportunities. My hope is to inspire others to embrace their own gifts—whatever they may be. Practice them, enjoy the journey, stay focused and commit to the process. I truly believe that in doing so, you'll find peace in your efforts.

This is my first attempt at writing. It has been humbling. I have purposely not included certain parts of my personal life in this memoir. Two of the most obvious subjects I consider personal are politics and religion. A heart is rarely changed once a religious belief or political party loyalty has been established. I have wasted countless hours arguing with both religious and political zealots. In the end, nothing was gained except hurt feelings and anger. While interacting with patients, I routinely avoided engaging in these kinds of discussions, whether I agreed or disagreed with their comments or observations. I have seen firsthand how disagreements about who should lead our nation have torn apart friendships and even marriages. Whomever we, as voting citizens, elect to political office is a reflection of the majority and our nation as a whole, for good or bad.

I was born and raised in a sick, racist, and segregated Memphis in the 1960s. People like myself and my generation have worked long and hard to ensure that our children and grandchildren don't have to endure the ugly and dehumanizing face of racism. Along the way, I have become somewhat cynical. I cannot and have no desire to change another individual's socio-political or religious viewpoint. It's personal. Except when it impacts the lives of others.

My siblings and I spent our entire adolescence and young adulthood attending Providence A.M.E. Church every Sunday. I no longer consider myself a religious individual, but I do think of myself as being spiritual. I have always tried to live by the Golden Rule and treat other people, even strangers, as I would like to be treated. The mission trips I took with Doctors Steve Cole and Lawrence Madlock were not religious but felt spiritual as we treated patients in underdeveloped countries on the other side of the world. Similarly, I feel a sense of spirituality every time I treat low-income, uninsured patients who need my professional service but have nowhere else to go. To me, the difference between being a religious person and a spiritual person is clear. I am no longer a fan of following religious rules and rituals or attending church on Sundays, but I find peace and deep connection while serving my community. I still admire people who do attend church. It is my hope that we all make personal decisions to create pathways that lead to becoming better human beings and loving our neighbors—all of our neighbors. Those pathways are different for everyone.

I have tried to highlight those facets of my experiences that may be inspirational and helpful to others. After reliving my life through this memoir, I have concluded that my pathway has indeed been extraordinary. I feel very grateful for my accomplishments and for being in a position to inspire and encourage others. A *New York Times* film crew came down to interview me and others who have led extraordinary lives, and it was one of the first times I had considered my life from this larger perspective. I knew I had healed people through medicine, touched them through music, and inspired them through athletic feats. But to think that my *life* was extraordinary—that was a moment that made me proud and humble at the same time.

Of course, that doesn't stop me from dwelling on my mistakes, missed opportunities, and "What ifs." As I have spent weeks and months reflecting on this memoir and this life of mine, I can't help looking back and pondering what if I had done this? Why did I—or didn't I—do that? I have had the time to reflect on how different my life might have been if it had taken different paths. What if I had chosen MIT over Notre Dame after high school? What if the fibers in my quadricep had not torn and I had competed in the 1968 Olympics? What if I had become a Rhodes Scholar and studied at Oxford University. What if I had tried out for an NFL or CFL team (upon graduating from Notre Dame in 1969, both the Saint Louis Cardinals and Toronto Argonauts extended invitations for me to compete for a wide-receiver position)? What if I had become a full-time musician and not an eye surgeon? I sometimes feel as though I have led the life of two or three different men.

If there is one common thread connecting the different facets of my life, it has been music. Whether it be performing, practicing, or recording music with my saxophone, music has been my most consistent and ever-present passion. It provided stress relief after a long day of work. It became a welcomed companion when I was alone. And it allowed me to collaborate with other musicians, many of whom are lifelong friends.

Yes, there were some difficult times and poor decisions along the way, but I have had the incredible fortune of unwavering support in my life: from my mom and dad, from Rhynette, from my siblings, and from my many friends. For that, I am forever grateful.

A LIFE IN FOCUS:
PHOTOS AND MEMORIES FROM THE JOURNEY

First track ribbons as a 10th-grade student at Manassas

100 meters in Stuttgart, Germany

Olympic Trials 100-meter semifinals behind Olympians Jim Hines and Charlie Green

John Carlos and me representing the United States in Austria

Anchoring a winning 4x400-meter relay

Winning the 60 meters at Madison Square Garden

Anchoring the winning 4x100-meter relay at the 1968 Colonial Relays

Winning the 60-yard dash inside the old Notre Dame Fieldhouse

Notre Dame mini-reunion, 2023. Art McFarland, Don Wycliff, Dan Saracino, me, and Francis Taylor

Visiting Ole Skarstein in Bodø, Norway

My friend, Dr. James Williams, MIT professor

Rhynette and me with President Bill Clinton at the 1998 White House Christmas event

Rhynette and me with Vice President Al Gore and Tipper Gore at the 1998 White House Christmas event

Rhynette and me

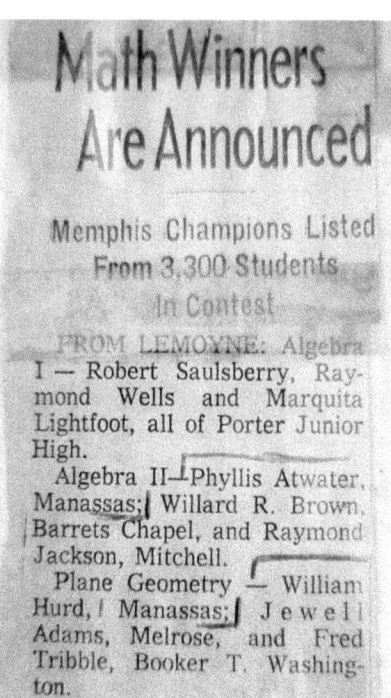

Memphis Press-Scimitar article: Winning citywide math contest

Performing at Germantown Performing Arts Center (GPAC), 2023

Rhynette and me

My sister, Mildred, and my son, Bill Jr.

Rhynette and I visiting Ryan in front of the National Stadium (Bird's Nest) in Beijing — site of the 2008 Olympic track and field events

Grandson Carson at age 5

Grandson Carson at age 15

With golfing buddy and author, Dr. Ferrell Varner

Lunch with Olympians Rick Wohlhuter (Notre Dame teammate & 1974 Sullivan Award winner) and Dave Wottle (Germantown neighbor)

In L.A. with my son, Ryan, and my twin first cousins, Carol and Catherine Branham

Performing at a Memphis event

Enjoying early fatherhood with Ryan

On the road with the band, Tom Lonardo, Sydney Kirk and Errol Thomas

Meeting Olympian Carl Lewis

Meeting Hank Aaron

Rhynette being appointed as Circuit Judge by TN Gov. Bredesen with Ryan and Bill Jr

My grandson Carson, competitive swimmer

My ace and ND classmate Dr Bob Cann

Meeting ND Football coach Marcus Freeman

Manassas Sprinter Tops Jesse Owens

Manassas High School sprinting specialist William Hurd has topped one of the records of the fabled Jesse Owens.

Hurd, a 17-year-old senior, was clocked in :09.3 in the 100-yard dash during a triangular track meet at the Fairgrounds yesterday, bettering the national high school record of :09.4 shared by Owens and three others.

Hurd's mark won't go down as a new record because he wasn't competing in a state elimination meet —that is, the district, regional or state high school finals.

Hurd's efforts in the 100 and also in the 220 and the low hurdles overshadowed the fact that his team finished second to Melrose in the three-way competition. Melrose had 64 points, Manassas 58 and Booker T. Washington 44.

In another Negro Prep League track meet, Father Bertrand scored 57 points to beat Douglass with 47, Lester with 33 and Patterson with 27.

Margaret Valiant Praises Example of William Hurd

Swift commendation is due young William Hurd, 17, described in Saturday evening's paper as a "Manassas senior, (who) would rather be a fine mathematician than the world's fastest human."

For too long our most gifted young men of the South have chosen to run the fast race in athletics, rather than the longer one in deeper studies. None can blame them for preferring the fast buck to the slow equation, for that's what the Alumni paid for!

Let's hope other youngsters will follow the Hurd example—and many Alumni also.

MARGARET VALIANT,
371 N. Willett, Memphis.

Memphis Press-Scimitar article April 1965

My homies, Dalton Hooks, me, Thomas Jackson,
Ed Prudent, Rudy Myers and Willie B Love

Rhynette and me

Golfing buddies Dr Steve Cole, Dr Joe McLaurin, me and Atty Clarence Halmon

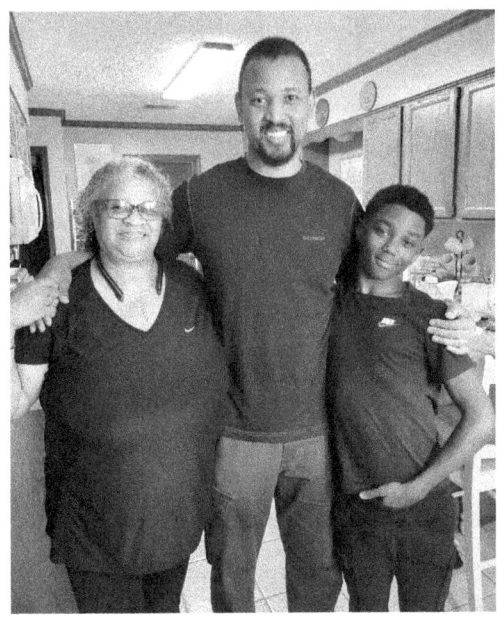

My sister Mildred, my son Ryan and Mildred's grandson Caleb

My sister Avar's older son Will (Pooka) and his family

My sister Avar's younger son and 2-time Grammy nominee Chris James

Sons, nieces & nephews: Mia, Ryan, Bill Jr, Will, Chris and Ashley

My sister Avar, her husband Bill James and his sister Bernice

1989 with Dr Manus Kraff (Clinical Professor of Ophthalmology at Northwestern Medical School) teaching me how to ski in Park City, Utah

With Rhynette, Yvonne and Lawrence Madlock in Maui 1991

The women in my family: sister Avar, mother Doris, niece Ashley holding son Ashton, wife Rhynette and sister Mildred

With 2 special people: Dr Mark Walsh and Dr Jan McWilliams

Signing a letter-of-intent to attend Notre Dame. May 1965 Memphis Press-Scimitar

AWARDS, HONORS, AND DISTINCTIONS

Throughout my life, I have been honored with numerous awards recognizing my achievements in athletics, music, academics, and service through medical missions across Africa, Asia, and Latin America.

ATHLETIC & ACADEMIC HONORS

1968: UNIVERSITY OF NOTRE DAME ATHLETE OF THE YEAR

Awarded to the most outstanding athlete at Notre Dame for their performance, leadership, and contributions to their sport.

1969: RHODES SCHOLAR FINALIST

The Rhodes Scholarship is one of the most prestigious international scholarship programs, awarded to individuals demonstrating outstanding intellect, character, leadership, and commitment to service.

1969: NCAA POSTGRADUATE SCHOLARSHIP TO COLUMBIA UNIVERSITY

A highly competitive award granted to student-athletes who excel both academically and athletically, supporting their graduate education.

1977: FIRST PLACE—STUDENT RESEARCH DAY AT MEHARRY MEDICAL COLLEGE

Recognized for presenting the top research project among medical students, demonstrating excellence in scientific inquiry and contribution to the medical field.

MEDICAL INNOVATION & SERVICE

1986: GRANTED A U.S. AND FOREIGN PATENT ON A SLIT LAMP MOUNTABLE INTRAOCULAR BIOMETER

A unique medical patent for an ophthalmic device that enhanced precision in eye examinations and intraocular measurements, improving patient care.

RECOGNITION FOR CAREER, CIVIC, AND LEADERSHIP ACHIEVEMENTS

1992: HARVEY FOSTER AWARD—NOTRE DAME ALUMNI ASSOCIATION

Receiving the Harvey Foster Award at halftime of the ND football game with Bill Jr., Notre Dame Alumni Association Executive Director Chuck Lennon, and President Joe O'Neill – September 1992.

Established in 1982, this award is given to a Notre Dame alumnus who was a student-athlete and has distinguished themselves through civic or university service.

1994: NCAA SILVER ANNIVERSARY AWARD

Honors individuals for their collegiate athletic achievements and their professional, charitable, and civic contributions over the past 25 years.

Awarded to six outstanding student-athletes from the Class of 1969, including Kareem Abdul-Jabbar (UCLA), Calvin Hill (Yale), Leroy Keyes (Purdue), Jim Ryun (Kansas), and Lee Evans (San Jose State).

1997: DISTINGUISHED BLACK EXEMPLAR AWARD—NOTRE DAME

Awarded alongside Condoleezza Rice, this recognition honors Black Notre Dame graduates for their exceptional leadership and accomplishments.

2000: FRAZIER THOMPSON PIONEER AWARD—BLACK ALUMNI OF NOTRE DAME

Named after Frazier Thompson, the first Black Notre Dame graduate (Class of 1947) and Monogram winner.

Recognizes Black Monogram Club members who have made outstanding contributions to diversity and inclusion.

2000: DELIVERED THE 8TH ANNUAL EMIL T. HOFMAN LECTURE AT NOTRE DAME

Established in 1993 in honor of Dr. Emil T. Hofman, a revered Notre Dame chemistry professor and dean.

Given by notable alumni physicians who have made significant contributions to medicine.

2002: 'MOOSE' KRAUSE AWARD—NOTRE DAME MONOGRAM CLUB

Monogram Club President Jim Carroll, presenter Bob Minnix, Krause Award recipient Bill Hurd, and Monogram Club Vice President Dave Duerson.

The highest honor awarded by the Monogram Club, named after Edward "Moose" Krause, a legendary three-sport athlete, All-American, and former Notre Dame athletic director.

Recognizes Monogram winners who have distinguished themselves professionally and through service.

2002: NOTRE DAME COLLEGE OF ENGINEERING HONOR AWARD

A prestigious honor recognizing outstanding achievements of Notre Dame alumni in engineering-related fields.

MUSIC & CULTURAL ACHIEVEMENTS

2014: W.C. HANDY HERITAGE AWARD—BEALE STREET MUSICIANS

Named after W.C. Handy, the "Father of the Blues," this award honors musicians who have made significant contributions to blues and jazz music, particularly in Memphis.

2014: INDUCTED INTO THE MEMPHIS SPORTS HALL OF FAME

Recognized for outstanding athletic achievements and contributions to sports history in Memphis.

2014: *A LIFE JOURNEY TO EXTRAORDINARY*—RECOGNIZED BY *THE NEW YORK TIMES* IN COLLABORATION WITH HOLIDAY INNS

Featured for a lifetime of extraordinary achievements spanning medicine, music, and athletics.

2016: SPIRIT OF HARMONY FOUNDATION SINGRING AWARD

Presented by pop artist Todd Rundgren, this award recognizes individuals who have made outstanding contributions to advancing music and music education.

Previous recipients include President Bill Clinton.

UPCOMING & ONGOING DISTINCTIONS

2025: KNUTE ROCKNE SPIRIT OF SPORTS AWARD (TO BE PRESENTED AT HALFTIME OF THE PURDUE–ND GAME ON SEPTEMBER 20, 2025)

Awarded to individuals who exemplify excellence, leadership, and sportsmanship in the spirit of legendary Notre Dame coach Knute Rockne.

PRESENT: ALL-TIME UNIVERSITY OF NOTRE DAME RECORD HOLDER—100M (10.2) AND 200M (20.4)

Holds Notre Dame's all-time fastest times in the 100-meter and 200-meter sprints.